VLAD
THE IMPALER

AND MORE EPIC TALES FROM DETROIT'S
'97 STANLEY CUP CONQUEST

- KEITH GAVE -

FOREWORD BY SLAVA FETISOV, HOCKEY HALL OF FAME

Cover design: Praveen Chukka
Inside cover design: Patrick Earl Alvarez
Interior design: Allan Nygren

ISBN: 978-1-952421-25-9

First Edition

Printed and published in the United States of America.

Visit our website at: www.keithgave.com
Contact the author at: keith@keithgave.com

This book is available in quantity at special discounts for your group or organization. For further information, contact the publisher at media@keithgave.com

Teufelsberg Productions
PO Box 302
Prudenville, Michigan 48651

For Volodya

Table of Contents

Eight weeks ago he lifted the Stanley Cup above his head. Today he struggled to lift his chin above his shoulders. Yet there is hope. I saw it as he struggled to answer the command to throw the little rubber ball. There was the determination, but the glint was gone from his eye. Eight weeks ago we watched for the next crunching check. Today he is strapped to a wheelchair sitting in the evening sun, and we cheered when he tried to place a baseball cap on his own head. Yet there is progress, though not like the newspapers suggest, not like all of us would hope. He is still fed through a tube protruding from his side. He had some ice cream—just a tablespoon or two. Maybe in a week or a month he will be able to eat baby food. Maybe in a month or maybe a year, he will walk or stand. It is still too early to tell, but he will do it if anyone can.

~ Jim Bellanca, Jr., 1997

Author's Note

Newly minted Stanley Cup champion Vladimir Konstantinov's hockey career ended abruptly when a weed-smoking limo jockey with a suspended driver's license fell asleep at the wheel and crashed into a large maple tree along Woodward Avenue in suburban Detroit.

Just entering the prime of his career and recognized as one of the best defensemen in the National Hockey League, Konstantinov suffered spinal cord and catastrophic brain injuries in that June 13, 1997, single-car collision that left him with the cognitive function of a small child. But considering the odds doctors gave him to survive his injuries that kept him in a coma for several weeks, the fact that he can speak a few words, get around with the help of a wheeled walker, and recognize some teammates, friends, and loved ones in his life before the accident is in itself more than a minor miracle.

But now one of the most beloved sports figures in Detroit's history faces another catastrophe, his survival hanging in the balance, thanks to unconscionable legislation passed by lawmakers on both sides of the aisle bought and paid for by the breathtakingly greedy Michigan insurance industry.

We can help.

Konstantinov, now in his mid 50s, requires around-the-clock care and supervision by a staff of health-care professionals that had been available to him—at least until July 2, 2021—under what was once model catastrophic injury coverage that made Michigan a leader in the nation. That ended when a new law, supported by Republican majority leaders in Michigan's House and Senate and signed by Democratic Governor Gretchen Whitmer, left thousands of victims vulnerable to losses of care they cannot afford.

They include Vladimir Konstantinov, who, 25 years after his playing career, is hardly rich. He never signed the kind of multi-million-dollar per-season contracts many elite hockey players enjoy today. The accident prevented that. Now those close to him, including family friend and retired attorney James Bellanca, Jr., of Grosse Pointe, worry that if Konstantinov loses that care and ends up warehoused in a nursing home, as happens to similar victims in other states, he may not survive. Bellanca witnessed it firsthand in the early years following the accident when Vladdie was removed from a rehab setting and briefly institutionalized.

"He did not fare well there. He was not comfortable in that situation," Bellanca said. "He's amenable to treatment from people he knows, but breaking into a new routine is very, very unsettling for him. Look, not everybody can handle Vladdie. He's a strong man and a very strong-willed person. He's also a gentle giant, but at the end of the day he does not take change readily. What people don't understand is that the only way he's going to be treated in a setting other than the one he is in now would be in a nursing home—warehoused in a room he would probably share with another person, without supervision.

"And the only way he can be controlled is either tied down or doped up. He needs activities. As a result of his injuries, he doesn't have the ability to make decisions for himself. Left unattended, he will hurt himself."

Konstantinov lives in a condo in West Bloomfield, Michigan, where a staff of caregivers help him eat, bathe, dress, and venture out into the community. He was a frequent visitor to Joe Louis Arena, where he occasionally sat in his old stall in the locker room while his former teammates prepared for their games. He occasionally makes special public appearances, such as the premiere of *The Russian Five* documentary film and Red Wings-sponsored ceremonies like retiring jersey numbers and the final game at The Joe. Always, he seems to be healthy and content, smiling from his wheelchair and shaking hands with friends. His handshake remains as strong and full of life as it did on the night when he and his teammates ended a 42-year drought by winning the Stanley Cup a quarter-century ago.

But that entire lifestyle is now threatened by legislation passed in 2019—and that took effect in July 2020—guised as a bill to lower insurance rates at the expense of those catastrophically injured who depend on the kind of care Konstantinov and 18,000 other victims in Michigan need to survive.

The new bill allows for drivers to carry as little as $50,000 in personal injury coverage to save money. Conventional insurance policies typically provided $250,000-$500,000 in such coverage, sums that could easily be exceeded by an extended stay in a hospital's critical care unit following a serious-injury accident. But the trade-off to save a few bucks is extreme. Some call it cruel and heartless.

We should help.

A major provision of the bill slashed reimbursement for such care by 45 percent, meaning that money paid from the Michigan Catastrophic Claims Association for things like physical and occupational therapy, attendant care, nursing care, and medical supplies is being cut nearly in half. And it's not like the state can't afford it.

A month before the new law took effect, the Michigan Catastrophic Claims Fund, something that every insured driver in Michigan paid into for years as part of their no-fault policies, had $23.4 billion in assets with liabilities of about $21 billion to be paid out over future years.

"The money is there," Bellanca said. "That's why this is so abominable."

It's worse than that.

"This is a money grab—at the pain and expense of 18,000 survivors. It's that simple," said Tom Constand, president of the Brain Injury Association of Michigan, who is striving to overturn the legislation—or at least amend it to protect those who were dependent on the funds prior to the new law taking effect. That's probably the most heartless and despicable thing about the new law: it's retroactive.

"Who's going to look those people in the eye and tell them that the care they've already paid for, that has allowed them to live the life they've been living, is suddenly being taken away from them?" Constand asked. "They contracted for that care in their policies. This is callous. This is cruel. It's a humanitarian crisis of care."

Why? Because the insurance companies want that money. "The end game is the $23 billion," Constand said. That kind of money buys lawmakers who need it to keep getting re-elected to enact laws that are far from the best interests of the constituents they so callously misrepresent. Four months after the law went into effect, health-care administrators were still trying to assess the damage as reimbursements from insurance companies were paying pennies on the dollar.

"It's just a shit-show, to be honest," said Linda Krumm, Konstantinov's medical case manager for the past 20 years. "We're all kind of holding our breath right now. A lot of home health-care agencies have closed. They just can't do it anymore with the cap that limits the amount that's reimbursed.

"We're just taking it month by month going through this. My company has already been affected. I'm not getting paid on certain things, but our clients are so dependent on us. We keep going, hoping that things change."

That's what drives Constand, who worries that the law is destroying the residential rehab healthcare provider industry as we know it. In just a few months, 1,500 workers lost their jobs.

"We should have been proud of our system in Michigan. It was an economic engine, providing jobs to get people the care they desperately needed," he said. "Am I optimistic? I've gone beyond optimism. I'm just determined to have legislation be heard and passed this year, before the end of (2021)."

Help, in the form of restoration of rightful benefits, cannot come soon enough for survivors. Constand compared brain injury patients to those who take blood-pressure medication to stabilize a heart condition. "The longer you go without treatment, the more they will regress—and you start going the other way quickly," he said. "And now the clock is ticking."

We must help.

How? For starters, raising awareness and raising hell, which is in part the point of this book project. If people indeed get the leadership they deserve, then we need to change our leaders in Lansing because there is no way we deserve this. We are better than this.

In the meantime, we can contribute to the Vladimir Konstantinov Special-Needs Trust, a GoFundMe account established by his daughter, Anastasia, to help with incidental needs. As of this writing, monies were barely trickling in, falling far short of what he may eventually need.

A portion of the proceeds from the sales of this book will go to the fund. I also plan to sell off three of the whopping four memorabilia items I collected (actually purchased at fundraisers) during a career of more than 40 years of writing about sports.

At a charity bowling/silent auction event to raise money for the education of the children of my great friend and Detroit Free Press colleague Corky Meinecke, a victim of cancer at age 45, I was the highest bidder on a few items: a signed game-used Easton hockey stick from Slava Fetisov; a signed game-used Easton hockey stick from Vladimir Konstantinov; and a white Red Wings No. 16 (Konstantinov) jersey—new, never worn—signed by each member of the Russian Five just a few weeks before the Stanley Cup playoffs began in 1997.

I am actively soliciting bids, and when someone offers me a number I cannot refuse, I will donate every penny to Vladdie's trust. (I'm keeping my Louisville Slugger signed by Al Kaline.)

The way I see it, it's the least we can do for Vladdie, someone who gave us so many thrills, who sacrificed so much of himself to help get the Detroit Red Wings, finally, to the Stanley Cup summit again.

#Believe

Foreword
by Slava Fetisov

I remember coming to the United States as a young guy with my dream of playing in the Olympics in Lake Placid, New York, and representing my country, the Union of Soviet Socialist Republics, the USSR, with the greatest hockey club in the world. And we wound up in prison.

That's how it was in the Athletes' Village. We slept in double bunks in tiny rooms—-cells actually—with no windows and a metal floor. And I was thinking, *This is the United States of America?* It felt more like a third-world country with watchtowers all around us and barking dogs all day and night so we couldn't sleep. *What kind of country is this? Maybe all those things we were taught in our history books in Russia were true. Maybe the USA wasn't such a great place after all.*

And then somehow we lost to a bunch of college kids on Team USA—yes, it absolutely was a miracle!—and we returned home in disgrace with a bronze medal. But in the end, we know now, Soviet hockey can take credit for the remarkable growth and popularity of hockey in the United States.

You're welcome, America.

My career with the Soviet National Team and the Central Red Army Club continued, and I was eventually named captain of both teams. I took my leadership role seriously, and I began to fight for our rights to pursue our careers outside Russia. Some of us wanted to test our skills in the National Hockey League, the greatest league in the world. But the Soviet system was like an iron fist, and we were treated like slaves in a grueling eleven-month season with barely one month away from our own hockey prison to spend with our families.

Eventually I beat the system, but it took a lot out of me. Again I entered the United States, the most democratic country in the world, with new dreams, only to be discriminated against wherever I went, even in my own locker room, for just one reason: because I was born in Moscow, Russia.

I had two choices: fight through it or go back. Do you realize how hard it is when you don't speak English and some guys are talking and laughing, and you cannot help but think they must be talking about you? This was tough. So you might understand why, when I arrived in August 1989 to join the New Jersey Devils, hockey was kind of secondary—and I have to admit as well that the Stanley Cup was not a priority.

Then I started to travel with the team, and I saw these great towns and cities all over North America, the beautiful hockey arenas, the five-star hotels. I slowly began to understand. The English started to work for me, and I learned about the people, Americans. I got the feeling for their history. I started to see them in a different light. Soon I began to understand what a great country this is. (Even if the Athletes' Village in Lake Placid eventually did become a prison that actually houses New York criminals.)

And when I went from building to building and saw the jerseys hanging up at the top, I started to think that I was involved in something big. I began to understand that this is a man's game, and this is the price men pay to be No. 1 in the world.

I learned that the passion and patriotism, the hopes and dreams of North American players and their families were just like we shared in Russia when we were competing for Olympic gold, World Championships, and Canada Cups. And it occurred to me that someone out there was trying to separate us as people, that we were all brainwashed by the propaganda.

I saw people stand up and hold their hands to their hearts, and I understood that this was something very different from what I experienced in 1980. And I knew then that the Communist propaganda—and American propaganda too—was wrong. What I was taught was not how the people of the United States really are. It was time to throw that history in the garbage.

At the same time, the other players, and especially the fans, began to see us Russians for who we are: hardworking and decent people who share very similar hopes and dreams for themselves and their families. And we could help their team win too.

Suddenly, after battling through all the discrimination and hatred and unwarranted physical abuse while the Canadian referees turned the other cheek to allow it to happen, it struck me how fragile our world is. Yet there we were, especially a few years later in Detroit, guys from several different countries playing the toughest game on the planet, sweating and crying and together spilling our blood on the ice, laughing and talking about our families and kids over a couple of beers. And then you realize—or certainly I realized—this is more than just a game we are playing.

I have had the honor and privilege to win just about everything a team can win in hockey. I played more than 1,800 games as a professional. I was very successful, with fans everywhere. I can go anywhere in my country and be recognized. People shake my hand and thank me for what I have done for the Soviet National Team and the Red Army Club. This is something money cannot buy.

But the old Soviet system, the way it treated the players, was terribly wrong and broken. I remember the first time they said I could go to New Jersey to play in the National Hockey League. They said, "You're going to make a lot of money, and you're going to bring your paycheck to the Soviet Embassy. You can keep a thousand bucks and the rest goes back to the government." When I asked why, they said, "Because the Soviet ambassador doesn't even make so much money." And I said, "Well, then let the ambassador play the hockey in New Jersey, okay?"

So I didn't go. I wasn't going to be treated like a slave, to be bought and sold. Instead I challenged the system. It was a time that scared me to death, but eventually I got my passport. This was my fight for democracy, for the freedom of choice that most Soviet citizens never experienced. Soon, more Soviet players were leaving. Sergei Fedorov was the first in Detroit, followed by my great friend Vladimir Konstantinov. Slava Kozlov was next, and I joined them when the greatest coach, Scotty Bowman, made a trade with New Jersey in early 1995. That autumn, Scotty made another trade with San Jose to get Igor Larionov.

And then we were five.

Along with so many other outstanding players in Detroit then—like Steve Yzerman, the great captain, and Nick Lidstrom, and others who would soon come, like Brendan Shanahan and Larry Murphy—we became a powerful club. And 20,000 of the happiest people in the world were going crazy every time we played in the Joe Louis Arena. Then in 1997 we were finally able to give them the Stanley Cup. They had been so patient and loyal for so long—and we did something special for them.

It's funny, when I think of it now, that when we went to the White House to be greeted by President Clinton, there was only one guy, Dougie Brown, who was an American. One Yankee! The rest? From all over Canada, Russia, Sweden.

So in my mind, Detroit was a great example of what America was all about. Some of the best and brightest people from all over the world want to come to the United States—scientists, educators, and even hockey players—for the chance for something better. And all those great minds and talent helped build the most powerful democracy and economy in the world.

Most important of all, however, is that we began to know one another, to understand each other as people. Detroit is the greatest example of this, and that's why I insisted to NHL Commissioner Gary Bettman in 1997 that we bring the Stanley Cup for the first time to Russia and introduce it to our hockey fans there, especially the young ones.

Since I returned to Russia in 2002, I have come to appreciate that for all my accomplishments in the game, the thing I am most proud of is my international experience, because I *know* how important it can be to help build a better, stronger world. For seven years as Minister of Sport in Russia, everything I did was to grow the game of hockey—and all sports—for our young people and to promote exchange programs throughout Europe and North America so they can experience some of the things I did. And more recently, as a Senator in our government, I am trying to persuade my counterparts in Washington, DC, to promote policies that encourage international opportunities for young athletes.

With the situation we have right now in the world, I think the more we can be friends, the better our world can be. It's important for Americans to know that Russians are not aggressive. We are never the aggressors. Just consider our history: Napoleon tried to get us. Hitler tried too. We know how to defend ourselves. And then there is hockey, the roughest sport in the world. In hockey you have to play aggressively, but you can also play artistically. The Russians tried to bring something different to the world of hockey in the NHL, and the result was good. People around the world appreciated it. And we learned from it.

I know for a fact that if our kids become friends, then we have nothing to worry about. We just follow their steps. And speaking of future generations, it is now my honor and duty, after answering President Putin's call to join the Russian Parliament, to serve as Polar Regions Ambassador for the United Nations Environment Program (UNEP). Our main initiative is called The Last Game, an exhibition hockey game to be held at a base near the North Pole. It was scheduled to be played in April 2020, but because of the pandemic we have had to postpone it. We are hoping we can involve some of the sport's greatest players as well as bring many world leaders to the event to draw attention to the plight of the fragile arctic ecosystem.

We are facing an ecological catastrophe. The polar ice cap is melting like ice cubes in our hands. We must put our political differences aside and think about our children and grandchildren. We must save our planet for upcoming generations. Many of us remember something called "Ping Pong Diplomacy" that opened relations between China and the United States in 1971. I like to think of this event at the North Pole as "Hockey Diplomacy," to unite people from around the world against climate change for the next 30 to 40 years, enough time to give Mother Nature a chance to recover.

This is my new challenge. And this is what I believe sports can do for our world right now. It is a wonderful way to bring people together. We need to build more bridges than weapons. That is my sincerest feeling about what can happen between our countries, Russia and the United States, and countries around the world at the moment of extreme need.

It is my greatest hope, and I know it can succeed. We made it work in Detroit, where it all started, where we built a beautiful bridge.

Viacheslav Alexandrovich Fetisov, "Slava" to his legion of friends and fans, is one of the most decorated players in hockey history. The Moscow native was regarded by many as the best defenseman in the world for much of the 1980s. He helped the Soviet

Union win the gold medal at the 1984 Sarajevo Olympics and again at the 1988 Calgary Olympics, finish first seven times at the IIHF World Championship, and win the Canada Cup in 1981. Fetisov was also named player of the year two times in the Soviet Union while playing for the Central Red Army Club from 1976-77 through 1988-89, winning the Soviet Championship League title in all 13 seasons. As a member of the renowned Russian Five, he helped Detroit win back-to-back Stanley Cup titles in 1997-98. He was inducted into the Hockey Hall of Fame in 2001. He is now a member of the upper house of the Federal Assembly of Russia.

Introduction

While I am immensely proud of The Russian Five franchise—the documentary film and the book of the same name—I'll be the first to admit I was misguided as both projects were coming together. I lost countless arguments over the several years that our film's production team was putting the story together. If I'd had my way, it would have been a four-hour box-office bomb rather than the award-winning 100-minute picture it turned out to be. As I often told folks wherever I've been invited to speak, all the good stuff we couldn't fit into the film, so many extraordinary details and memorable anecdotes, were in the book.

Well, I was wrong there too.

To be perfectly honest, if I'd included everything I felt was worth sharing, instead of 316 pages, *The Russian Five* book would have made Tolstoy's *War and Peace* seem like a novella. So, with the 25th anniversary of that glorious season upon us, this book, centering around that 1997 Stanley Cup championship team's most endearing and charismatic character, aims to correct that. Vladimir Konstantinov remains among the most respected and beloved athletes in Detroit's fabulous sporting history, and it seems like everyone has a story about him. This book allows them to tell their stories in their own words.

But there was so much more to share about this team. While researching and writing *The Russian Five* and interviewing myriad players, coaches, and others central to their epic story, I filled two large bins with material. And every time I moved those heavy containers, from the cabin on my beloved trout stream in northern Michigan to the tropics of southwest Florida and back to Michigan on a lovely lake where I now call home, I heard voices from within those bins screaming to be heard, clamoring to be let loose to tell tales that must be told. This book, in other words, aspires to unveil the rest of the story around that special season. And it does so in the words of those who were there, right in the middle of it all—Hall-of-Famers and grinders—unabridged and lightly edited.

After a career of sweating out stories against brutal deadlines for a couple of America's great morning newspapers, I've come to actually embrace and enjoy the process of writing, But I'm convinced that even if I could recall the spirits of Steinbeck and Hemingway, of Tolstoy and Dostoyevsky, of Pushkin or Poe, I could not improve on what these Stanley Cup winners offer in their own words. So, with a few notable exceptions, I simply turned them loose and got the hell out of the way. I hope you enjoy it half as much as I did as I sifted through thousands of pages of notes and interviews for some gems that celebrate a memorable time in Detroit Red Wings' history.

Finally, I confess that this book, like *The Russian Five*, is yet another kind of love letter to one of the best men I've ever known and a player with redoubtable Hall of Fame credentials, Vladimir Konstantinov. But this project goes a step further. So it is that my sincerest gratitude extends to everyone who buys a copy of this book because a share of proceeds from sales will go to financial resources established to ensure the continued care and well-being of Vladdie at the time of his greatest need.

It's All in the Name

He was born in a city far above the Arctic Circle, where summer is barely a rumor and the polar night lasts 40 days, from early December to mid January, a place Mother Nature conceived especially for the sport of ice hockey, the game he was destined to rule.

They called him Vladimir. Perfect. A name composed of the Slavic *Vlad*, meaning "to rule" and *mer*, "great, famous," according to renowned Russo-German linguist Max Vasmer,

Vladimir Nikolaevich (son of Nikolai) Konstantinov. More than likely, his parents and close friends called him Volodya, or Vova, or perhaps even Vladmirko—diminutives, little terms of endearment the Russians embrace. As we do when might use Bill, Billy, or Will in place of the more formal William.

Nicknames are often substitutes for proper names of people familiar to us, or ones we enjoy having in our lives even from a distance. But places or things count too. Pucks and nets are often called biscuits and baskets, eh? And we fondly remember The Joe, even if Joe Louis Arena was a second-rate venue for hockey even on the day it opened.

Our nicknames for people are often used to express a kind of affection, compassion, tenderness, or respect. According to a study by Bellevue University in Nebraska, men give nicknames as a way of being affectionate without compromising masculinity. So it's no wonder in consummate team sport like hockey that NHL locker rooms cannot exist without them. Virtually every member of the team has at least one moniker.

The most common among them involve adding a "y" or "ie" at the end of a name. Steve Yzerman was commonly referred to as Stevie by his teammates, though some who admired his skills called him Silk. The rest of us know him as The Captain. Brendan Shanahan was Shanny. Bob Probert was Probie. Joe Kocur, Joey. Slava (a nickname in itself for the more formal Vyacheslav) Kozlov was Kozzie. Igor Larionov was Iggy to his teammates, The Professor to the rest of us. Slava Fetisov was Papa Bear to everyone, though these days as a member of the Russian Parliament we address him starting with The Honorable.

Sergei Fedorov, certainly Seryozha or Seryozhka to his loved ones, was usually called by his given first name or Feds by his teammates. Most often, though, they just passed him the biscuit and got out of his way.

But Vladimir Nikolaevich Konstantinov? Now there's a guy with some nicknames, all of them reflecting some measure of admiration, respect—and even fear. At first we knew him as Vlad, or Vladdie. Then we watched him play, and if he didn't lead the league in penalty minutes for his transgressions, he certainly had more handles than most players—many of them, frequently used by opponents, aren't suitable for widespread reader consumption.

He's probably most widely known among Red Wings fans by the melded version of his name and a popular hero from an action-movie franchise, flicks he watched on his arrival in Detroit that helped him pick up a few words in a new language. I mean, how could we not smile and love him more when he slipped the shades over his eyes and promised, "I'll be back!" with a flawless Arnold Schwarzenegger accent.

That's when he became The Vladinator.

But there were other candidate nicknames tossed about as he made his reputation as one of wickedest competitors in the game. Call him dirty; we can live with that and he could too. He played to win, and if he had to bend some rules in the corner in a scrum for the puck, or if he was indiscriminate about who he leveled at center ice with a bone-crushing (and sometimes career-ending) but legal hit, so be it. Hell, that's how Gordie Howe played the game, eh?

By the time he had emerged as one of the game's best defensemen in that magical 1996-97 season, Vladimir Konstantinov's reputation was taking on mythical proportions. And he had just turned 30 when his team went on its Stanley Cup run that spring of '97.

His most colorful nicknames often had a historical or mythical edge to them as well, like Vladimir the Terrible, a play on an actual Russian leader in the mid 1500s; Ivan the Terrible, a dangerous man known for inspiring fear and terror among enemies; or Vladimir the Great, a play on another Russian leader, Peter the Great, whose reign started in the late 1700s and included several successful wars that vastly expanded the Russian Empire (he also founded St. Petersburg).

But the best and perhaps most accurate of all of Vladdie's nicknames we borrowed for the title of this book: Vlad the Impaler, another renowned historical figure after whom Bram Stoker developed his literary Count Dracula character. That Vlad, a ruler in medieval Romania, was known as a man of unheard cruelty and justice. One legend about him involved Turkish messengers who went to Vlad to pay respects but refused to take off their turbans, according to their ancient custom. Not a problem, Vlad said. He then proceeded to bolster that custom by nailing their turbans to their heads with three spikes so that they could not be removed.

There is nothing on Vladimir Konstantinov's resume that suggests he could be that kind of cruel. To be sure, we know that however he might have used his stick as a weapon at times, he never actually impaled anyone. But ask anybody who ever opposed him on the ice, and they wouldn't put it past him.

Sorry, Little Brother

In his memorable Hall of Fame induction speech, Brendan Sha-nahan paid tearful tribute to his family: his father, Donal, lost far too soon to Alzheimer's Disease; his mother, Rosaleen, who in her 50s got her first driver's license so she could take her sons to hockey practices; and his three older brothers, Brian, Danny, and Shaun, who would become his greatest fans. Obviously, Brendan was their favorite NHL player—at least until he was traded to Detroit.

As Brendan tells it:

I don't know how Vladdie got those nicknames, but they were appro-priate. He was a dirty player. I hated him when I played against him, but I loved him as a teammate. My brothers hated him too—when I didn't play for Detroit. A month into my time there, though, I remember talking to them and they said, "We have a new favorite player, little brother."

When Vladdie was on your side, you *really* grew to love him. He was a very stoic guy, old-school Russian. He didn't speak a lot; he didn't show a ton of emotion. I remember we used to call him "Shark Eyes." There was just a blankness behind them when he would go out and . . .

do things. But he had a lot of skill too. He was a Norris Trophy finalist, but he didn't care if the game was 1-1 or 9-1 in the third or whether it was the other team's toughest guy coming up the ice or the other team's most skilled guy; he played one way from start to finish.

He was a great hitter, not an overly big guy, but there was just something about him that had great density. When he hit guys, he hurt them, and he went looking for it right up until the buzzer went. There were nights when we were up 6 or 7 to 1 against a less skilled team and we didn't really have a tough guy on the bench. We'd be sort of riding the night out, just wanting to get out of Dodge. The other team was embarrassed, and they wanted to get out of Dodge too. And with only about a minute or two to go, Vladdie would step up in the middle and catch a guy with his head down and either throw a hip check or just about knock him out and we'd be there on the bench thinking, *Oh man, these next two minutes are going to take about a half hour to play, because they're going to send out all their fighters now.*

But Vladdie backed it up. He didn't care and we never got mad at him because that was just him. And you know, I don't ever remember Vladimir Konstantinov not having some form of a cut or a bruise or a mark on his face at any point during the season. He never looked clean. But he was a pro, very low maintenance. I can honestly say, none of us knew him really that well off the ice. Vladdie was quiet. Like Slava [Fetisov] and Igor [Larionov], he was from the sort of Russian old school. I'd even put [Slava] Kozlov in that category, even though he was younger. Sergei [Fedorov] was definitely from the Russian new school, you know, the sports cars, the slick suits, the long, highlighted hair. But what was interesting is that both the old-school Russians and the new-school guys, they all loved Vladdie because he was what they epitomized as *the* Russian hockey player. You know, just get the job done. Don't talk about it; just be effective at both ends of the ice.

And the one thing I always thought was funny: With the great forwards he played with, guys like Larionov, Fedorov, and Kozlov, somehow it was always Konstantinov who got the breakaway, went forehand-backhand for a goal. With all the options of the guys on the ice, I don't know why it was always Vladdie who somehow broke free and got the breakaway. But it was.

He also threw a lot of hard hits. The one that's probably most memorable is the one that ended Dale Hawerchuk's career, in the Stanley Cup Finals, and led to a goal later on that shift. I think I scored it, but you know, it had thrown off the Philadelphia Flyers so much that they were just chasing him around. And we went up the ice and had a couple of shots on net, and I ended up behind the net and threw it out in front off of [goaltender Ron] Hextall's legs. Dale got up and finished his shift, but he never played another shift in that game, didn't play Game 4, and retired that summer.

It was just a classic, feet-on-the-ice hit with the shoulder. Vladdie was about the same size as Hawerchuk, but there was something about the way Vladdie hit you. That was not only one of the hardest hits I've ever seen him throw, but the timeliness of it, right at center ice against a superstar, and no penalty. Then the other team's chasing him around and as they're chasing him we're going up the ice on a three-on-one breakaway.

It's funny. I remember watching the replay of Game 1 after the playoffs were over. I forget who was doing the game, what broadcast it was on, but it was all about Eric Lindros and the Legion of Doom and the Philadelphia Flyers and how people like Mark Messier were saying, "It's your time now, Eric." The broadcasters kept talking about how big and tough they were and how they were going to run us around. And then you watch the first minute or two of that game—I think we started the Grind Line—and the commentators are all of a sudden quiet as we throw the puck in and—*BOOM!*—Maltby hits somebody. The puck goes D to D [defense to defense] and then—*BOOM!*—McCarty hits somebody. And the Flyers pass it up the wing and—*BOOM!*—Vladdie hammers him.

And in the first minute and a half, we showed we were quicker and heavier, meaner, and hit harder. And I forget the exact time of it, but at a certain point in all of this, you know, people are watching and saying, "What's happening here? I thought this was the soft, slick, Russian Five team?" And then one of the commentators says, "Well, you know, you can't underestimate how talented this Detroit team is as well. They have a chance here." It was like they were saying, "I guess we actually might not have paid enough attention to Detroit."

As it was, we swept the Philadelphia Flyers, and the series was never really in doubt. And not only did we win, we were able to beat them not only with skill, but we beat them physically as well. We beat them up. We won the Stanley Cup. And Vladimir Konstantinov was a huge part of that—as were all the Russians.

Who Stole the Zamboni?

As it is written in the NHL's book of records, the Detroit Red Wings won the 1997 Stanley Cup championship with a four-game sweep of the much-favored Philadelphia Flyers. But everyone on the Detroit bench knew it was over with about a minute to play in the second period of Game 3 at Joe Louis Arena—when eventual Hall-of-Famer Dale Hawerchuk lay at center ice, metaphorically impaled by a guy named Vlad. As teammate Brendan Shanahan noted, the Flyers were so intent on exacting some retribution by chasing Konstantinov all over the ice, three Wings charged into the Flyers' zone against one Philadelphia defender, and it didn't end well—for the Flyers. When Shanahan banked the puck in off goaltender Ron Hextall to make it 5-1, at that moment the outcome of the series was indisputable.

Dave Lewis, the former assistant coach, says so:

How much of a wrecking force was Vladimir Konstantinov in the Stanley Cup Finals? Well, he sure had some huge hits in that series.

It was funny at the time because we knew Dale Hawerchuk was fine (he finished his shift, but that was his final appearance in an NHL uniform), but someone joked on the bench that Al Sobotka forgot to take the Zamboni off the ice. The players could not believe that hit.

It sort of exemplified everything Vladimir Konstantinov stood for. Hawerchuk was a highly skilled guy. He was later in his career, but he had the respect of everybody in the league. But Konstantinov didn't care who you were or where it was; he played his game. And that was the epitome of his game right there. At the biggest moment in his hockey history, as far as a player goes—the Stanley Cup Finals—and he just freight trains this skilled player at center ice. It was right in front the benches. Our guys were going, like, "Wow!"

And, yeah, the Flyers lost their perspective on what's important.

When Vladimir Konstantinov hit Hawerchuk, it changed the game. It changed the series. The series was over at that point. They just had no response to Vladimir Konstantinov. There was nothing they could do. [Eric] Lindros couldn't do anything. None of their tough guys could do anything because it didn't affect Vladimir Konstantinov. His game was a game that nobody in the league played.

I don't know if anybody since has played the kind of game that he played. It was a special game, and I got to see it every day. Our players got to see it every day. Vladdie just played like that all the time, and the Flyers just didn't know what to do.

Genesis

Mike and Marian Ilitch put up the dough. Jim Devellano did most of the heavy lifting in scouting, drafting, and building a roster. And the players, bless their hearts, paid their dues in blood, sweat, and an ever-widening river of tears. There were others too, and frequently overlooked. One is the president of the Dallas Stars these days, and he wears a Stanley Cup ring from their title in 1999. But in the Red Wings' formative years after the Ilitches bought the franchise, they turned to their son-in-law to run the business—which included several cloak-and-dagger missions to free several players from behind the Iron Curtain and bring them to Detroit. Jim Lites doesn't get nearly enough credit for building one of the NHL's most powerful franchises—25 straight seasons in the playoffs, eh?—but in reality he was the great and powerful Oz behind the Red Wings' curtain.

●━━━━━━━━━●

Or, as Lites tells it:

I consider myself a Texan, and Dallas has been wonderful for me. I love Dallas. But Detroit is home for me. My family is there; two of my children grew up there. Detroit represents all the things I was able to do in my career. I went to law school there. I met my wife [Denise, the eldest Ilitch daughter] there. I got to work with the Ilitch family—and not just the Red Wings. While I was there we bought the Tigers. I found the FOX Theater when it was falling down and renovated it, one of the greatest things in my career, and 25 years later it's still the greatest theater of its type in the world.

Detroit represents many really positive memories for me. I started working with the Detroit Red Wings in 1982, first as a lawyer working on the outside for my father-in-law, Mike Ilitch. At the time, the Red Wings were a bankrupt franchise—in every sense of the word. They were beaten down. They were playing in a bad facility, Joe Louis Arena, that never had been completed. It was the most sterile building you've ever seen. It was unfinished. Fluorescent light bulbs were hanging on bare wires in the concourse. We set up card tables to sell merchandise. The locker rooms weren't done. There was no practice facility. It was just a mess. And no fans, maybe 3,000 season ticket holders and no excitement for the games. Then we had a roster of aging veterans and no prospects under an owner, Bruce Norris, who had run the franchise into the ground.

Mr. Ilitch basically took over something that no one would touch. It's hard to believe but he purchased it for next to nothing. It was losing money. It had an awful payroll. At one time they had 81 players under contract. And there weren't eight of them who were capable of playing in the NHL. So we bought that and essentially got a great trademark and logo in a great hockey market with an owner who *believed*. But he also knew exactly what he was buying.

The great thing about it? This was a franchise that we stripped right back to the floorboards, back to the studs as it were. We got to start from scratch. And it was great. If you ever had an opportunity to meet Mike Ilitch, you saw he brought an intensity to almost everything he'd ever done in his life. And he certainly had his passion with the Detroit Red Wings. I got to be the beneficiary of that when I was a very young man. Being part of it; getting caught up in Mike's enthusiasm in the marketing of the team; all that he thought he could bring to that process—that really was the groundwork.

It led to the unbelievable success the Red Wings had over the course of two and a half decades. It all began with Mike's purchase of the team and his hiring of Jimmy Devellano, the key hire for Mike and a really good decision. Mike had an understanding about what you have to do to win in the National Hockey League and it's true to this day: you have to draft and develop players. If you don't draft well, you can't be successful.

We interviewed three or four guys for the general manager's job, some of them in the Hall of Fame today, but Mike picked Jimmy because of how he helped build the New York Islanders. Mike would say, "Find me the best No. 2 guy out there, the guy picking the players for the best team." At that time it was the New York Islanders. They were in the process of winning four consecutive Stanley Cups. They had won 19 consecutive playoff series. They were a dynasty, which is why Mr. Ilitch ended up hiring Jimmy Devellano as opposed to several other really qualified individuals.

The first draft of the Ilitch-Devellano era was 1983. He purchased the team just before the 1982 draft, but he didn't control it, and Jimmy wasn't hired until a few months after that. The first Devellano draft was really the start of the Red Wings' dynasty. The first-round pick was Steve Yzerman. The second-round pick was a player named Lane Lambert, who had a very good career cut short by injury.

And the third-round pick that year was a guy named Bob Probert, who went on to great success and set the tone for toughness. Later [in the fifth round] the Red Wings drafted Joe Kocur, who was kind of a bookend to Probert. So we got the Bruise Brothers in that first draft.

The fifth player we got in that draft was a guy everybody knew was a great player but he was from Eastern Europe and therefore blocked by the Russians from getting out to North America, a guy from Czechoslovakia named Petr Klima, who was an all-world talent. Jimmy let one of our scouts, Neil Smith, have one pick, and Neil used it on Petr Klima. This was in 1983, if you can imagine, and we had a chance to see him in London [Ontario] with the Czech National Junior Team. It was very clear the guy had real talent, as much talent as any young player in the world at that time.

That started the whole process of, "We're going to do whatever it takes to get better as soon as we can." That's the dynamic that Mike Ilitch had. He basically said, "I don't know how to do this, so I'm going to let you run with it, Jim. Figure out how to get him over here." That was our thought process: We don't care where the players come from. We're going to use foreign players. If they're good, we're going to find them and we're going to bring them here.

That's how it all started—with Mike's energy, his commitment, his financial resources, and the love affair he had with the city of Detroit. And he fueled it with wild marketing ideas, like giving away automobiles. In a downtrodden Detroit auto market, he gave away an American-made car every game. Everybody thought he was nuts. But that's how he was. He wanted to remind people that the future would be better.

Where Only Winning Matters

Through much of his tenure wearing the "C" on his chest above the winged wheel, Steve Yzerman was considered among the greatest captains in NHL history, which qualifies him in redoubtable terms to speak to the importance of leadership—especially where real leadership begins. And in the Detroit franchise, he suggests, it began well above his pay grade.

Here's The Captain:

The general attitude or philosophy of the organization was dictated by the Ilitch family, and it was passed down to Jimmy D., to Scotty, and all the way down to the players. They were progressive thinkers. They were willing to try things, never afraid to try something different. If it didn't work, it didn't work, but let's try.

That philosophy probably led them to some decisions they made when they were drafting players. And look at what the Red Wings did in '89 with that draft [Nick Lidstrom, Sergei Fedorov, and Vladimir Konstantinov, among others]. It completely changed our franchise. We got multiple Hall-of-Famers out of one draft. That may never happen again.

The Ilitch family just wanted to win a Stanley Cup. They ran a great organization, but ultimately they were committed to winning. And they did what they had to do, starting with hiring the right people, like Jimmy D., Scotty, and Kenny Holland.

It started with the Ilitches right through to our players. It was always, "Guys, we are here to win." When we got to '95, '96, '97, it was all about winning. If you were there for any reason other than winning, you were not going to enjoy it. And you were not going to fit in.

A Draft for the Ages

The most successful business executives pay close attention to the world around them—social issues, the economy, politics, and global events. That includes sports executives. And in the late 1980s, Red Wings GM Jim Devellano, Executive VP Jim Lites, and their boss, Mike Ilitch, were paying attention. It enabled them to make some bold decisions—with more than a gentle nudge from their top scouts—that would transform the franchise almost overnight.

Here's Jim Lites:

The world was changing with [Leonid] Brezhnev out and [Mikhail] Gorbachev in [to lead the Soviet Union]. The United States announced the thawing of economic embargoes. There was a rumor that the Berlin Wall was going to come down. There was talk of reunification of Germany, with East and West becoming one.

All those things were the undertones leading up to our draft in 1989, when we said to ourselves, "If we don't pick good Russians now, we're never going to get them. We won't get a jump on everybody else." Mike was very interested in getting Russian players. And Jimmy D. had softened a bit on his position about relying on North Americans, particularly Canadians. We needed talent.

Neil Smith was then our assistant general manager, and he had a young guy named Ken Holland who would become our chief scout and eventually the general manager of the franchise. They had seen these young Russian players play, particularly Alexander Mogilny, Pavel Bure, and Sergei Fedorov. They thought that was the next generation of great young players—and we had better draft one or more if we were ever going to get this team where we wanted to take it.

That was the motivation that led up to it. Remember, we did it with Petr Klima, so we had a certain confidence level that we could do it [import Eastern European players] outside the political process—at least that was our hope, especially with the thawing of the political systems at the time.

There was a time, of course, with the Russians, when no player would even think about making the jump, because their family would be murdered. I had a conversation long ago when we were waiting in Germany with Klima. Nick [Polano] and I had a break. We had a month in Europe, so we went to a tournament in Switzerland. And we struck up a conversation with a guy named Igor Larionov, probably a 23-year-old kid in 1985 [actually 24 then].

Remarkably, there was no security at all around the Russians, so we laughingly said, "Come on. Get in the car with us and let's go. We'd love for you to play in Detroit. Come on, defect with us."

He looked at me and I'll never forget it. He spoke in perfect English: "Jim, Nick, not a chance. You know what would happen." And he drew his finger across his throat. "That's what would happen if I left." That was 1985. By 1990, the world had changed.

World politics were changing. Russia was changing; they were losing control of the republics. The Baltic states wanted out. Czechoslovakia was going away. All that Soviet underpinning was gone. The Russian Federation was still really powerful. They controlled every player. But the players now had a different attitude, a different approach, especially the younger players. They had an idea of what they wanted to be, and you could sense it. Our scouts and other people knew they had to get at this. That scenario underscored the 1989 draft of the Detroit Red Wings. Regardless of where the players were from, Mike Ilitch's desire was to make the team better. And our understanding of the system, everything we learned during the Klima defection, was all elements that were in play going into that draft.

The Detroit Red Wings in 1989, it was a great, dynamic group at the draft table led by Mike Ilitch. And I remember there was a certain amount of feeling that if we don't start taking these [Soviet] players earlier, other teams were going to start to do it. Until then, nobody had ever used anywhere near a high pick on a Russian player.

At the draft table and in scouting meetings, I was just an observer. I ran the business. So they would say to me, "Well, if we used these early draft picks on Russian players, can you get them out?" Their idea was that anything lower than a sixth-round pick was a high pick. "You've got to give us some comfort that you think you can bring them over." And to me, with everything that was going on in the world, it seemed like a wise thing to do, or at least try.

But it was kind of a funny draft. Neil Smith was announcing our picks, and I remember Jimmy Devellano saying, "Okay, I'll give you the third-round pick on a European." It's funny now because so many of them are in our league now, but it was risky then to take any Europeans, let alone Russians, as high as the third round.

We had taken two nice Canadian boys in the first two rounds, Mike Sillinger and Bobby Boughner, and both went on to have pretty good careers in the National Hockey League. Then we get to the third round, and Neil Smith picks Nicklas Lidstrom, a Swedish defenseman, if you can imagine that. Neil and Kenny were thrilled that Lidstrom had fallen to them in the third. I think Jimmy D. was surprised we didn't take one of the Russians. But Neil was worried that if they didn't take him then, Lidstrom wouldn't be around in the fourth round.

And then the negotiations really started, as heated as I'd ever seen around a draft table. "What are we going to do?" "What about the Russians?" "Are we prepared to take one now?" And Jimmy D. was saying, "No, I got a guy I want to take—Dallas Drake." Now Dallas Drake turned out to be a pretty good player, but Neil and Kenny were saying, "Jimmy, there are Dallas Drakes all over the place. We want one of these Russians."

Remember, Mogilny had been drafted the year before by Buffalo, and there were rumors that he might be leaving [defecting from the Soviet Union] and that Buffalo was going to get him. And there was some talk that people weren't sure that Bure was even eligible to be drafted—some technicalities in the draft year based on his age and international experience.

But they knew Fedorov was eligible, and I remember Neil and Kenny imploring Jimmy Devellano, saying, "If we can find a way to get him out, Sergei Fedorov is a top-three forward in the entire world." Jimmy again acquiesced, basically saying, "Go ahead, but I don't want to hear about any more Europeans after this."

And with the fourth pick, Neil stepped up and took Sergei Fedorov, the highest a Russian had ever been taken—by several rounds. Now I didn't know Sergei Fedorov from anybody. All I knew was, if these guys, who I knew and trusted—like Kenny Holland, Neil Smith, and Christer Rockstrom, our head European scout—were this excited about these players [Lidstrom and Fedorov] then they had to be pretty good.

We came to the fifth round, and Dallas Drake was still there, and

Neil Smith was still imploring Jimmy D. We were killing it in this draft, doing great. I didn't know if Dallas Drake was ever going to play in this league, but the other Russian was still there. We should take Pavel Bure. But there was still the question about whether he was eligible.

Our guys were saying, "I want to take Bure. If he isn't eligible, we'll get some sort of compensation later. It's not our fault; we thought he was eligible." But Jimmy D. was adamant: "I told you guys. I gave you the third and fourth picks. I'm taking the fifth pick." [Then Devellano chose a center named Shawn McCosh, whose NHL career consisted of one goal in nine games, none with Detroit, and who went on to make his fame as a middle school teacher in Phoenix, Arizona.]

Bure was still there in the sixth round and our guys were still hoping to get him. But it didn't happen. Three picks before our selection, Vancouver took him. The league said it would take it under advisement, and it turned out Neil and Kenny were right about Bure being eligible. And they were devastated.

With our sixth pick, Jimmy took Dallas Drake, who turned out to be a pretty good player. Not Pavel Bure, but . . . The rest of the draft continued on, and when we got to the late rounds, our guys were still disappointed that they had missed out on Bure. So we were in the eleventh round, and Jimmy D. said, "Are there any other Russians you might want to take here?"

So we took the captain of the Red Army team, Vladimir Konstantinov. He was a little older, an established player, a captain in the Russian military with a wife and a child. We had done all that research, and our guys knew him. But we thought that if there was ever a guy who would never come, it was going to be one of the guys hardened to the Russian system, a Communist. The last guy who was ever going to come was Vladimir Konstantinov.

You have to remember, Jimmy D. is an old-school guy. He has a way.

He believes you build a team with great North American players. Those are the guys who do it for you at the end of the day. He's softened over his career, obviously. He's seen how great the European players are, what they can add.

So right after the draft, he came up to me and said, "Look, I gave up that fourth-round pick to get Fedorov. Now it's your responsibility to get him out. *You* have to find a way to go get him out." And I remember saying to myself, *If I could get Klima out of Czechoslovakia in 1985, then I can find a way to get this young Russian player out.* So I told Jimmy, "It might take us a couple of years, but we'll get on it right away."

On the Art of Leadership

How do you lead a room full of leaders? Steve Yzerman showed us how: by embracing what many strong-willed teammates brought to the battle and sharing the mantle. In other words, he didn't gather followers; he created more leaders.

And, as usual, Yzerman understates his role:

Well, my role as captain on those teams was not that significant. We had several prominent guys, a lot of dominant, or strong, personalities. Very successful guys, very motivated guys, and they were all leaders in their own right.

There was nothing that I could say to Igor Larionov, nothing I needed to say. I admired him. And Slava Fetisov. What they had done as players, the way they conducted themselves . . . And we had Brendan Shanahan on that team. Nick was a little younger at that time, but there was nothing that I could say or do to help Nicklas Lidstrom. He's one of the best players ever to play the game.

And as for our Russian guys, they were good guys, they were good teammates, and we had a lot of fun. They had some independence.

What I liked about our team then is that we got to a point where we were all somewhat older.

Most of us had families with children. We were just very professional; we came to the rink and we played. There weren't a lot of petty jealousies; there were *no* petty jealousies. We had guys who were 35 years of age on that team who wanted to go out for dinner with the 21-year-olds. The younger guys probably didn't want to hang with us. We weren't that exciting. But everybody appreciated the differences—the different personalities, different ages, different backgrounds and cultures that everybody came from.

Every day when we got to the rink, we had a lot of fun. There was a lot of humor, a lot of banter. Whether you were a Canadian, American, Russian, or Swede, we were all at a point in our careers where winning was the most important thing. And I would credit Scotty Bowman for creating that atmosphere on that team.

He'd always say, "Guys, this is about winning." And everybody bought into that. So for me as a leader, it was just a matter of showing up, playing hard, working hard—and that was the way it was for everybody.

On the Russian Influence

What made The Captain such a great player, an extraordinary leader? Well, just about everything, according to those who got to really know him. Especially the way he embraced Russian players—as teammates in Detroit and as some of the most important players on the roster he built in Tampa Bay that eventually won back-to-back Stanley Cup titles. From helping build a dynasty in Detroit to watching the Red Wings dominate the league from afar after he went to Dallas, one guy saw it all.

Here's Jim Lites:

Steve Yzerman is the ultimate superstar player turned general manager. He always had a great sense of what was right, how to do things, and what it meant.

I think Steve knew that the Russian influence was the reason why the franchise had the success it did. He has always been great, but there were years when he and the team were up and down a bit. From about 1987 to the early 1990s, the Red Wings were a good team, and he was a great player on a good team. When he became a good player on a great team, they became Stanley Cup champions.

Steve realized that he never would have gotten there without that group. The Russian Five were the reason they won the Cup. There are always players you need on a championship team, certain levels of players. But the Russian influence made Detroit, to me, along with Nick Lidstrom—that European influence—so great

Everyone who has success is copied. We're no different than any other business. Whatever is successful is emulated. So of course teams started scouting Europe heavily. Hey, why buck the system? The teams, in my opinion, that aren't open-minded about where they're going to get their talent are the teams that aren't successful. Certainly it's been true my entire career. We've had unbelievable success in Dallas with European players.

Look at the Colorado Avalanche in the late '90s. Look at the New Jersey Devils throughout their runs, and Pittsburgh with Evgeni Malkin, Washington with [Alex] Ovechkin. One exception might be the Chicago Blackhawks with a little less European influence. But there are teams that don't do it, some [general managers] with loud mouths who say they have to win with North Americans.

That's a bunch of bullshit. It really matters to be broad in your view. Detroit with the Russian Five was the first completely amalgamated team. They had a great Canadian leader in Steve Yzerman, and a lot of great North American players. But the icing on the cake was what the Russians did and how they did it, the level and depth they gave to that team.

Even then the North American players in Detroit were adapting their style. They had every base covered, and that's why they were two-time champions—three times in six years and eventually four times over a number of years. They were able to sustain unbelievable success with all that infrastructure they built.

I'm sure everything those Russian players did rubbed off on their team. And it rubbed off on all of us. *All* of us in the National Hockey League were impacted by the great work the Russians did over here—and what they collectively did as part of the Russian Five in Detroit.

A Victim of Unintended Consequences

One player on the bloated, ugly roster the Ilitches inherited when they bought the team stuck around long enough to become a vitally important foundational piece – a fixture for years on Steve Yzerman's left wing. But he too eventually found himself out of a job in Detroit – a victim of the Red Wings European invasion. He was also smart enough to understood he was witnessing the evolution of the world's best hockey league, and he harbored no resentment.

•━━━━━━━━━━━━━━━•

Here's Gerard Gallant:

When I was drafted by the Red Wings, it was different ownership. Then when I signed my first contract, Mike and Marian Ilitch had just bought the hockey team and they were great with me from day one—great owners and great people.

And Jimmy Devellano was given the green light to go get some great hockey players. I remember my first year there might have been 3,000 people in the building. They were giving away free cars to get people to come to the games. It was unbelievable.

My first couple of years here we had long stretches of not winning games. We were losing twice a week by scores like 1-5, 0-8. But we were able to build some character early on. We brought in guys like [Bob] Probert and [Joe] Kocur, Shawn Burr, Steve Chiasson, a bunch of these different type of hockey players. They were all good hockey players, but we were a blue-collar team. We worked hard and we battled hard, but we still weren't good enough. Then the players we got from Sweden, from Russia, from around Europe, they made our team a lot better in a hurry.

I think it was awesome that we went all in with the European players. As players, all we wanted to do was win. It didn't matter where the guys were from. We just wanted to win and have a championship team. When we got some of these players coming over from Russia, Sweden, our team definitely changed for the better.

If there was talk around the locker room about Europeans being soft, that you can't win if you have too many of them, I never heard any of that. At least it was never said around me. When we got those players, we knew we were a better team. Guys like Nick Lidstrom, [Sergei] Fedorov, [Vladimir] Konstantinov, and [Slava] Kozlov—they made our team into an elite hockey team. We still had a little ways to go, but they made our team a lot better.

Toward the end of my career, I sort of got pushed out from those guys coming in, but you know what? It was all positive, because those guys were great hockey players, so talented. And they made the speed of the Red Wings that much better. We had a tough, physical team when I was there with Probie and Kocur and all those guys, but we weren't quite the Stanley Cup championship team like we were going to see in the next 3 to 4 years after that.

Love at First Sight?

The Soviets had been playing hockey for only a decade or so before they brought a team over to North America to play a pretty good junior-level team with Scotty Bowman behind the bench. He didn't much care for how his team was manhandled in that first game, but he sure admired how the Russians did it—with a very different style of hockey.

Here's Scotty Bowman:

The first time I ever saw Soviet hockey, it was with an all-star junior team in Ottawa. I was assistant coach, and we had a game with the Soviet National Team. That would have been in 1956, so they only started hockey maybe ten or eleven years before that. They were older than us. Our players were all under 20, but a number of them would go on to play in the NHL.

And the Russians, their equipment was pretty ragged. We were wondering how they were even going to play the game. Well, they really opened our eyes. We got beat 1-10. It was hard to believe. I mean, we never had the puck. That was the first team I ever saw that really exploited the long, long plays—and the way they were anticipating each other.

Then we played a second game in Montreal, and we recruited some stronger players from other teams. We lost that game 3-6. In the early '60s, probably around '63 or '64, I was coaching a junior team in Montreal—another team of good young prospects. [Goaltender] Jacques Plante had been retired from the NHL for a couple of years. He was working for Molson Brewery and he heard about the game against another national team of the Soviets and volunteered his services. Well, Jacques stood on his head—and we beat them 2-1.

Then they had the big series in '72, the Summit Series. I didn't get involved in that, but it was a great series. If you check the stats, you could tell they played a different style. Their forwards would take over [the defense] when one of their defensemen had the puck. We never did that in the NHL. Our NHL defensemen in that series were really good, with guys like Brad Park, Serge Savard, Guy Lapointe, and Pat Stapleton. They were all really good two-way defensemen. But when they played the Russians, they didn't get many points because they were always wary of those long plays.

And the Russians, their game was all offense. They didn't worry about defense. They didn't worry about checking. Their idea was, they were going to have the puck. I don't know if they were that good without the puck, but they were terrific when they had it.

And NHL teams at that time were not at the same level of fitness. When I was coaching in Montreal, we had a super team, and the Soviets, every player on their team tested in the 70s [VO2 max]. We had only one guy, Guy Lafleur, who was super-conditioned, at that level. Bob Gainey was in the high 60s. But we had some guys in the 30s. The big difference was the conditioning. And that's what happened in '72. The Canadian team was really good, but it took them a couple of weeks to get going. And they played their best hockey in the final four games of the series.

Another thing about the Russians when we played them, they always wanted to dress two extra players because they wanted four units of five, or twenty skaters [with two goaltenders]. When I started coaching in the NHL, we had sixteen, then later eighteen like today. So I was a three-line coach when I started.

But the Russians wanted the same defense pair with the same forwards. They never worried about power plays. They didn't mix different players from different lines. Their five-man units played together. I used it a little later, but it's harder to do that in the NHL with three pairs of defenseman and four [forward] lines. Unless you didn't want to play one of the lines, it was hard to match up.

Bowman Takes Control

In his second year in Detroit—after that crushing first-round playoff loss to upstart San Jose, the eighth seed against the heavily favored Red Wings—Scotty Bowman demanded more control of the roster. He wanted to determine which players deserved to be in Detroit and which would be sent to the minors. More important, he wanted the authority to make trades so he could secure the kind of players he felt he needed to win.

The Wings' hierarchy was skeptical; after all, Bowman's roster-building acumen was anything but a rousing success in his seven seasons as general manager in Buffalo. Owner Mike Ilitch eventually acquiesced, but he ordered Jim Devellano and assistant GM Ken Holland to try to keep Bowman on a short leash. They tried, contesting Bowman's efforts to trade for a couple of older Russians. In the end, Ilitch authorized the deals.

Good call, eh? Otherwise the Wings might still be trying to figure out how to win a Stanley Cup.

Here's how Devellano remembers it:

In 1990, we brought in Bryan Murray to be our coach and general manager, and he did a nice job getting our team kind of rolling. But we had some playoff disappointments. It was probably more the makeup of our team. We were an offensive team, but our owner Mike Ilitch wanted a coach who could win in the playoffs.

And, of course, we were able to bring in Scotty Bowman, and that's exactly what happened. We also gave him more authority than a normal coach; we made him our director of player personnel, and he had a big impact—like trading for [Slava] Fetisov and [Igor] Larionov.

Well, then we had five Russians on our team, and the rest is sweet history.

What did those two bring to our team? I'll tell you. They brought three things: respect, respect, and respect. Sergei Fedorov was beholden to those two guys. If they told him to get his ass in gear, Fedorov got his ass in gear. It wasn't only Scotty now. Scotty had a couple of allies. And Larionov especially was a good conduit to Scotty Bowman. It was almost like he was a coach, a mentor, for the younger guys, Kozlov, Konstantinov, and Fedorov. They were young kids and they looked up to these older Russian players. They knew those two were superstars in the Soviet Union. That really helped our club.

A third of our team were Europeans, and five were Russian. Now the pride factor kicked in. It was like, "We're going to show these people in North America we are great. They can see we've taken the Canadian game to another level."

Different Yes, But Not Soft

Fans, often influenced by misguided media, are all too quick to label certain players as "soft." Even coaches will occasionally whisper the word in background conversations with reporters. But the truth is, for even the very softest of players, it takes more courage to skate a single shift in the NHL than most of us can muster over a lifetime.

And yes, that word "soft" was once used ad nauseum by North American players to describe the invaders from Europe who came to steal their jobs. Detroit's Russians, and Swedes like Nick Lidstrom, Tomas Holmstrom, and later, Niklas Kronwall put an end to that kind of talk forever.

Take it from Steve Yzerman:

My perception of Russians and Russian hockey in general was, I never considered them soft by any means. It's true they came from a different culture, a different way of thinking. When those guys started to come over, they were leaving a Communist country that had a very different ideology, different values.

They were just different. They grew up in a different system, and as a result they thought differently than us. Those guys were never soft, but it was an adjustment for them.

I talked with Igor [Larionov] a lot about it. He and Slava [Fetisov], the older guys, would tell us about training for eleven months a year with no time off. Igor talked about how they got one night off to go home after they won the Olympic gold medal. One night to go spend with your wife—but be back in the morning, you know?

They wanted to come here because there's so much more independence, much more freedom for them. And that's an adjustment too for the younger players in particular. You come to a completely foreign country. You don't speak the language. You have so much more freedom. That's hard enough for those of us who grew up here ourselves.

Just imagine, put us in Russia as 20-year-olds with no parental supervision. We don't speak a word of Russian, but we're free to just go out and do our thing. That's a lot for a young person to take.

Russian hockey players were always admired for their skill. These guys are tremendous athletes; they're well trained. Their strength, their skill, their speed, their skating ability—those were the things that stood out.

But it took some time for them to adjust, and looking back on it, that's to be expected. In Tampa Bay we had several Russian players too, and those guys were our most dedicated, most professional guys on the team. They were able to make the adjustment. And the five Russian players we're speaking about in Detroit—those guys are a big reason why the guys in Tampa were able to make that adjustment. The guys in Detroit led the way.

When you're living with these guys every day, you see how important it was to them. The one thing about Russians that I've learned from being around them in hockey is, they're very, very proud. And in particular the older guys, Igor, Slava—they were extremely proud.

I think the younger guys, Slava [Kozlov], Sergei, and Vladdie, they were watching the older guys and seeing how important this was to them. I know they talked about it, and for Igor and Slava, this was really important to them. They had won a lot. They had accomplished a lot. But they had something to prove by winning [in North America].

They're proud hockey players, proud of where they come from. Whether they defected or had to negotiate with their government to come over here, they're still very proud to be Russian. And you see now, they all go back, and they speak proudly of Russia. They still want to represent Russia; they haven't lost that.

What they all went through, the way they conducted themselves, the way they played for our team, and the way they evolved, it has really changed the tone for European players in general. After the Russians, we had the Swedish players all come in. Nicklas Lidstrom won the Conn Smythe Trophy, and he was the first European to captain a Stanley Cup team.

So the perception of all European players, it's just evolved. But the first group, the Russian Five, they were probably the biggest leaders in that change.

Cold Welcome for Europeans

North American players, especially those from Canada, didn't exactly roll out the red carpet during the mass migration of players from Europe that began in the late 1980s. Nicklas Lidstrom was one of them, along with Swedish teammate Tomas Holmstrom and the five Soviets who joined the Red Wings. Detroit, of course, led the way adding imports to its roster, which may be why the environment was a bit different in the Wings' dressing room compared to the rest of the league.

Here's Nick Lidstrom:

I didn't feel that resentment in our locker room, but I felt it around the league when we were playing other teams. Being from Sweden, sometimes they would call you "Chicken Swede." Or sometimes I'd hear from other players, Swedes on other teams, that North American players were worried that Europeans were taking their jobs.

That happened a lot early on when more Europeans were coming over, especially when the Russians started coming over in the late '80s, early '90s. It took a few years before that kind of faded away. After a while, they saw us more as teammates, helping the teams instead of taking their jobs.

But certainly, I could feel that resentment early on in my career.

Redbird One's First Mission: A Defection

Denise Harris was hired in 1990 as the chief flight attendant and office manager for the Ilitch organization's newly formed Aviation Department—and does she have some stories to share. Some of them, like spiriting away defecting hockey players, she can even tell on the record. Fasten your seatbelts!

●————————————————●

Here's Denise Harris:

Well, on July 1 we started the Aviation Department for the Red Wings. Mr. Ilitch was out in the hangar, looking at his plane and everything, and he came up to me and said, "Hey, kid, I have our first mission for you, our first flight." And I said, "That's great, sir. Where are we going?" thinking maybe he wanted to go to Italy, or maybe Florida. No, he said, "Kid, we're going to go kidnap us a hockey player!"

And I thought, *This is going to be the greatest job of my life. This is going to be wonderful!*

He didn't say a whole lot more about it. We knew that they had drafted Sergei Fedorov and were interested in getting him. But they kept the flight crew a little bit in the dark regarding the initial logistics of it, what they were really doing. We knew we were going there to try; we didn't know if it was going to be successful or not. We also knew Sergei was young and he didn't speak much English.

On July 21, we made our flight plans to go out to Portland [Oregon]. I asked, "How many people are going? How many are coming back?" Because I had to work on the food and logistics and what everything we needed. And they said, "Just worry about one player." And I'm like, "Well, what does he eat?" You know, I've got to take care of this person properly. It was a very trying time, and they said, "Don't worry about him. He'll eat whatever we have on board."

So we flew out to Portland, parked the aircraft, and they said, "We could be back in an hour. We could be back in a few hours. Just keep the plane running and we'll call you when we're on our way. We're going to get Sergei and we're going to get out of here as fast as we can and take him back to Detroit." So, that's as much as we knew.

And we sat there with the unit running. We told air traffic control that we were going to stay out there and that we were going to take off as soon as the business meeting was over. And we waited . . . and waited.

There was a lot of excitement, a lot of positive energy. But there were undertones of "Man, what if this goes south? What if this goes off the rails?" Because they didn't know for sure what was going to happen. Sergei was young, you know? Was he going to continue on his journey with us, or was he going to continue on with the Goodwill Games and leave us hanging there? And as a flight crew, we were just happy and proud to be part of it. You don't get to do that too often.

Well, we got word that they were coming. They called right after they got in the limo. So we were like, "This is a go!" You know? We got everything ready. We even pulled chocks from the plane. We had the ground crew out there ready to flag us out, and we notified the tower that we were leaving very rapidly. Our plan was to get off the ground as quickly as possible because we had no idea if the police were going to be following them, or if they were going to put a stop on us from taking off.

All of a sudden here comes the limo, and out comes this beautiful, smiling young man. Sergei just looked like he was ready, you know? And Jimmy [Lites] was smiling too. But we just wanted to go, you know? We were fueled, watered, everything. Close the door, let's get out of here!

When I saw Sergei, I immediately felt this strange motherly connection to him. He was so young, and he looked . . . he was very happy. He was smiling, but I could tell he was a little nervous about what was happening: What did he leave behind? What was going to happen back there? I just felt this protective feeling over him, and I have no way to really explain that, besides that I just wanted to make him feel comfortable, make him feel welcome, take away any worries he may be having at the time, and let him enjoy his ride back.

But he was very gracious, smiling. Of course he didn't speak much English, but he dropped the F-bomb; that's the only thing he could say, for the most part. But we were communicating just like you would think, you know? I had magazines with pictures, basic body language communication. I had magazines like *Sports Illustrated*, the Detroit papers, the *News* and the *Free Press*, *USA Today*, so he could become more familiar, more comfortable with where he was going.

I think he was a little overwhelmed and just needed to sit and settle in and think about what he did. So my service at that time was to give him his space and let him come to me if he needed anything. He was watching everything that was going on around him. I think he was analyzing the heck out of everything and everybody.

Sergei was very, very well mannered, very polite, and he's a very smart man. People underestimated his intelligence, and I think that's exactly what he wanted people to do. He measured people, their character. And eventually he totally embraced America, the culture, the food, and yeah, the red Corvettes, the nice suits. He always presented himself very well. He was happy.

Second Mission:
Get Vladdie

*Immediately after they had Sergei Fedorov safely in Detroit, the Red
Wings intensified their efforts to somehow, some way get Vladimir
Konstantinov out of the crumbling Soviet Union too. It would
prove to be much more difficult because Konstantinov, the captain
of the Central Red Army Club, also held the rank of captain in
the Soviet military under a 25-year contract.*

*Before he could even dream of defecting, he had to secure his dis-
charge from the Army. But even then, he wasn't leaving without
his family: his wife, Irina, and his young daughter, Anastasia. So
the Wings had their work cut out for them. Eventually, with the
help of their Russian agent, Valery Matveev, a former sports-
writer, they hatched a plot to get Konstantinov out of the military
by spreading Mike Ilitch's money around among several doctors.
One of them demanded—and received—a big new American car
for his false prognosis that Konstantinov was dying of cancer and
could no longer serve effectively as a soldier, let alone play hockey.*

*Ultimately, it worked. Barely. And just over a year after Fedorov's
arrival in Detroit, Konstantinov and his family escaped by train
to Hungary, where they were met.*

Flight attendant Denise Harris picks up the story:

We got a call from Mr. Ilitch, who basically said, "We're doing it again! Only this time we're going to take this show international." I said, "What are you talking about?" and he said, "We're going to Budapest, and we're going to have one of the other Russian hockey players come with us."

So now we're all pros at this, right? We were so excited. This time it was going to be Vladimir, his wife, and his daughter. I asked Sergei what he thought: Was there anything else we could do? How did his flight go? Was there anything we could do to make Vladdie and his family feel more comfortable?

Sergei said, "No, he's fine." And I'm like, "Come on, help me out here, buddy." But he didn't offer any good suggestions. I guess he figured he had to suffer through it, so Vladimir was going to have to suffer through it.

So we get on the plane, and we fly over to Budapest. We didn't know all the problems that were happening on the back side, only that they were coming into the city via train. And again, we were thinking we didn't want any . . . I mean, now we're involved in an international kidnapping defection? I'm wondering, *Do I have a KGB file going now?*

We were really proud of ourselves. Again, we were ready. It wasn't as dramatic as in Portland, where we were in the cloak of darkness with the plane running and all the lights out. This was during the day and once they crossed the border into Hungary, we pretty much had a little buffer to get him on the plane and everything like that.

But best laid plans, you know? I was briefed that Vladimir didn't speak any English, but his wife did. She was going to be acting as the interpreter on board. I was excited about that because it was a long flight to get back from there. Then there's drama. Here comes Vladimir and Jimmy Lites, but the others are staying behind. Irina and the daughter cannot come with us, and Vladimir had to make a decision.

I mean, could you imagine in the moment having to decide whether to go on? I have more admiration for this woman, his wife, for saying, "You go. I'll be okay. You're with good people." She trusted the Red Wings' organization. She knew Vladdie was going to be fine and safe. But you could tell he was distraught at his wife and child being detained. And one of the guys said to Vladimir, "We need to get going."

I could tell it was a struggle for him. I mean, I cannot even imagine being there in a foreign country, you're going to take off for a new life, you're going to defect—and you leave your wife and your child behind with people you don't really know. I just can't imagine how difficult it was. I looked at Vladimir, and I could see . . . I mean, he was a very strong, stoic man, but I could see on his face that he was worried, and he was conflicted like any good husband and father should be.

So we were really wondering, *Is he going to not go?* He wanted to stay with them until their visas, or whatever it was, their paperwork was straightened out. But he had to be convinced that he needed to go. And again, he wanted to stay with his family. His wife, being the strong woman that she was, had to convince him that she was going to be okay and so was their child. She had to talk him into leaving and going with us.

She had to tell him, point blank, "Vladimir, go. You have to go. We'll be fine." And Jimmy [Lites] was saying, "Trust us. We're going to take care of your wife and your child." But I mean, why should he trust us? Why? We were "kidnapping" him in a foreign country. I mean, it's a big leap of faith. It took a lot of courage. And it took a lot of courage on her side. I admire her. She pushed him to leave.

She said, "You go. I will be okay. We want this life. We want to go this

way. You're going to be in the NHL, and we're going to get to America."
Were they scared? I'd bet my bottom dollar they were petrified. Did she
let on? No, she did not. She was very strong. And I think because of her
he got on that plane and he left with us.

Vladimir was a quiet man, a man of few words. He was sitting there,
looking out the window, looking at the sky and just staring off. I could
tell he was worried. What man wouldn't be worried? I don't even think
it was that much about the hockey at this time. It was about his wife and
his child. Were they going to be alright? So I tried to do what I could do,
a little standup comedy routine, make jokes and try to make him laugh.

I had some sports magazines. I think Sergei happened to be on the
cover of one. So I picked it up and said, "Sergei." And he's like, "Yeah."
And I say, "Sergei big and strong." And he goes, "Psh." Then I said, "Sergei ladies man." Vladimir started laughing and tried to say something
like, "No. Sergei *thinks* he's a ladies man." I was just trying to engage
him in any way I could because he spoke very little English, just trying
to loosen it up a little bit.

Everybody else on the plane was sleeping. They were all tired, but
Vladimir couldn't rest. He was a little restless. I didn't sleep. I didn't nap.
I just stayed ready to give him anything that he may have needed at the
time, or try to answer any questions he may have had. It was tough for
him. I just felt a heaviness. Unlike Sergei's [defection], where he was all
smiles and ready to go and the energy was upbeat, this one was a little
bit different kind of energy. It was a little more sad.

Thank goodness it was a good ending for him.

No Crooked Pocket Squares

The former Soviets who came to Detroit to join the Red Wings weren't just world-class hockey players; they were great people—kind, polite, generous, grateful. They were also impeccably dressed.

●────────────────●

Denise Harris saw it on every flight:

The Russians were always so appreciative of everything that the Ilitch family and the Red Wing organization would give to them. They couldn't believe the plane; it was so beautiful. And they would help take care of it; they would always clean up after themselves. A lot of the others wouldn't.

And they were so gracious, always "Thank you" and "May I?" They wouldn't presume to go into the galley as if it was their own plane. They would think that it was my place and that they needed to ask permission. They wouldn't just walk into the flight deck, because that's the pilots' place. They just had etiquette—and gratitude for everything.

If I had given them a bowl of dog food, they probably would have said, "Thank you so much. This is wonderful," without even looking at it. But what I could see about the Russians, especially on the plane, was that they couldn't believe the gifts that this organization was providing the team—especially considering where they came from. I mean, Sergei would talk about the planes over in Russia. As we know, that one flight over there went down with [former Wings player and assistant coach] Brad [McCrimmon] on it. Stuff like that, because there were no regulations. And then there were the buses and the awful hotels.

Here they're in the top hotels, like The Drake [in Chicago]. Great hotels in every city, with great food. And they're being catered to on a plane, with great food. It wasn't airplane food, you know. We had four-course beautiful meals for them. Anything they wanted on the plane was theirs. And if we didn't have it, we'd make sure we'd go out and get it for them. So they could say, "Hey, I need a Snickers bar," and you better have that Snickers bar for them. It was like—*poof!*—magic. We made it appear for them. So, yes, the Russians were a little, like, shocked.

And they dressed well too! Vladimir and Sergei. They both rocked some nice Armani suits. The players still had to dress up nicely to fly, even on their private plane, which some of them were a little curmudgeonly about. They said, "This is our private plane. We don't have to go through the airports anymore, right? So why do we have to dress up?" Well, because it's part of the culture of the NHL, so just shut up and put your nice Armani suit on.

This was a plane full of beautiful hockey players, great guys, and they all were dressed nicely. It was hard to stay focused. They all got, well, in my book there were a lot of 10s. With the polished shoes, and the pocket scarves—they were very classic. And they made me want to dress more classic as their flight attendant. The flight crew wore suits too, and I always worried that my pocket scarf was a little crooked. And they'd say, "Oh, and you have a little scuff on your shoe." Damn. You don't want to be caught by a hockey player not looking your best.

Words You Don't
Say in an Airport

Of the five Russians who wound up in Detroit by the mid 1990s, only one spoke English before arriving in North America, and Igor Larionov spoke it eloquently. The other four struggled at the outset, but both Sergei Fedorov and Slava Fetisov, when he arrived in New Jersey, worked hard at overcoming the language barrier. Vladimir Konstantinov had the luxury of a teammate, Fedorov, who spoke passable English, so he took his time. And Slava Kozlov, as is his stubborn way, simply wouldn't be bothered learning a new language. He just shut up and played hockey. Want to speak with him? Learn Russian.

General Manager and coach Bryan Murray, in a stroke of genius, had Sergei Fedorov room with Shawn Burr, thereby giving the new Russian teammate a crash course in English whether he wanted it or not. Burr was one of the all-time media favorites in Detroit, first because he never heard a question he wouldn't try to answer, often in a colorful way, and second because he was a never-ending source of great jokes. (To this day, years after cancer claimed him in August 2013, we laugh when we remember him telling his trademark turtle joke.)

Here's how Nick Lidstrom remembers it:

S ergei had a good teacher in Shawn Burr, who liked to teach him all the bad words in English. It must have been hard, especially for the Russians, because they didn't learn any English in school. I had the advantage of learning the language when I was a young kid in Sweden, so I could get around with my English. But you could tell that the team accepted them right away, and they were trying to teach them some of the words and teach them kind of the culture of living in North America.

I remember Shawn telling Sergei as they were going through the airport, "Don't mention the word 'bomb.'" And sure enough, that's the only word Sergei spoke: "bomb." So security came and there was a big controversy about what was going on. Sergei didn't know better, but Shawn Burr was the jokester on the team, and he had a lot of fun with the language barrier.

But when they brought their play on the ice, that barrier kind of disappeared. Hockey is kind of a universal language, where if you play, if you read the plays and the other players are reading what you're reading, it looks like you're speaking the same language: the hockey language of knowing what to do on the ice. You saw that especially with the skilled Russians. You know they're smart hockey players. They know how to read plays, and the North American players appreciated that. They could see the skill and the smartness of the Russian players.

Lost in Translation

When it came to speaking English, his distant second language, Vladimir Konstantinov picked his spots. After all, why struggle for words when a grunt would do? Truth be told, he had a better command of the language than he let on, except for when he didn't want to be bothered.

●——●

At least that's what former coach Dave Lewis suspected:

When Vladimir Konstantinov first came to training camp with the Detroit Red Wings, the one thing that we noticed was how he played with the puck. It wasn't something we really expected. He had good vision. His compete level was really high. He had to go through the transition of playing on a small rink with bigger, stronger guys—not what he was normally used to playing against every night.

And the language was a difficult issue. I remember Vladdie coming to the bench his first year. We just got out of training camp, and I would say something to him in English like, "Good play!" and he would turn around and smile and say, "Yes." And the next day I might say something like, "Don't do that. That's a bad play," and he would go, "*Nyet*. Don't understand."

Scotty Bowman thought he understood more, and I agree with Scotty. I think he understood what he wanted to understand. As coaches we had to use the board an awful lot with them. We had to use video an awful lot—more so than with a North American player, and especially with the young guys who first came over.

That was different at the coaching level too. As a coach you say go do it, and they go do it. Now you had this language barrier, and it was a learning experience for me, using the board, video, taking them on the ice to show them positional stuff. You had to show them; you couldn't just tell them because they wouldn't understand. So it was a different mentality in coaching also.

But the swear words? Yeah, that was the first thing they learned. And Russian curse words were the first thing I learned too when I went to coach over there.

Yzerman vs. Fedorov?
No Debate

Shortly after the 1990 World Championships in Switzerland, Red Wings Senior VP Jimmy Devellano ran into captain Steve Yzerman, who was working out in the team's weight room. Yzerman had been voted the tournament's best forward; he scored 9 goals among 19 points in 10 games, though Canada finished fourth, failing to medal. The Soviet Union, led by its captain, Slava Fetisov (2 goals among 10 points and plus-20 in 8 games), won the gold.

But Devellano was interested in a young Soviet player whom the Wings had drafted the previous June. Yzerman and Devellano's conversation went something like this:

"So, Steve, what did you think of the guy we got on our list, Sergei Fedorov?"

"Oh, he's really good."

"Okay, but how does he compare to you?"

"Oh, he's better than me."

"Excuse me? Say that again."

"He's better than me."

"You're just saying that to be nice, aren't you?"

"No. No, I'm not. He's a stronger skater. He's better than me."

Suffice to say, Devellano was excited beyond the moon. "That's all I needed to hear," he said. "I couldn't wait to get him over here. I mean, if he was as good as Steve Yzerman, never mind better, we're going to be strong, strong down the middle."

And they were, but General Manager and coach Bryan Murray begged to differ with his captain's scouting report on Fedorov, a young center on that Soviet club who had 4 goals and 6 points in 10 games for the world champs.

Here's Murray's take:

When Sergei came in, he was a guy who could play against anybody on any team. Like Steve Yzerman, he often had to match up against the other team's best pair of defensemen. By bringing Sergei in, the other coaches had to make a decision.

Nevertheless, I don't think Sergei was better at that time than Steve. He was a very dynamic skater, and growing up in the system he was in, he knew how to play defensive hockey. He had a high skill level; he was one of those really competitive guys. He didn't want to get beaten by anybody, so I could imagine if Steve said what he said it was because Fedorov was a hard guy to match up against.

But Steve had other abilities. He had heart and soul, and he had the ability to find the open ice. These were two great players for us at the right time. But Steve Yzerman was the captain of the hockey team, no question about that. He had the room. He had the leadership ability. He had the core players and the veterans who understood that he was captain of the hockey team.

Sergei came in and he was very happy to be a good player on a good team. And when he went on the ice, he had great respect for Steve and would follow his lead.

What a Country! Both of Them

Maybe it was because they didn't know his language and couldn't figure out how to approach him in quieter times away from the ice, but Sergei Fedorov's teammates didn't exactly roll out the red carpet, at least socially, for him. Nobody said much about it, and Fedorov himself never complained, though every now and then he had some long meetings with his coach, Bryan Murray, expressing his frustration and trying to sort things out in his new country. Eventually the tension thawed, and Fedorov became just one of the guys—and often the life of the party. But it took some time. Denise Harris saw it all from her command post aboard the team plane, and it concerned her.

Here's Denise Harris:

It just appeared to me—because I was in the front and could see down the entire plane and I interacted with the entire plane—what I saw was that the other players were being not so inclusive to him. It hurt me, just as a human being, how they could be that way.

It wasn't everybody, but you could see it and you could feel it. I know he felt it, but he wouldn't say anything. Sergei, he just bought his time, showed them what he could do.

I think it was just some male bravado, you know? Something new, and I think they, a few of them anyway, were threatened by it. It wasn't overt; it was a little more covert—a little body language, just walking by him. But it was definitely something you could feel. They didn't know what to expect, and that scares people.

There were a few guys who were upset with Sergei coming in and having these things the Ilitch organization lavished on him. They didn't think he had paid his dues. They felt he walked into a goldmine and they were going to be put aside.

They just didn't know Sergei's side, what he had to go through. Again, it's a matter of communication and just asking. So I kept trying. I wasn't trying to be intrusive into their conversations, you know, on board, because that wasn't my position, but there are times when you have to speak up. And I took some of those moments. That's when I would say, "Why are you always looking at that side of things? Why don't you look at what he's bringing to the table, what he's bringing to the team, and what he's bringing to the city? And why don't you rise up and bring it yourself?

I'm not telling you what to do. I'm telling you how maybe it can be better, from my viewpoint. Because I see the whole 360 of your interactions, and I see the Russians over here at their table, quiet, and I see all you guys playing cards and jawing. There's something wrong. You're not cohesive."

But Sergei, he was always so happy, just the way he presented himself. His energy and enthusiasm for being here and being a part of it all—it was glorious to watch. It lifted everybody around him. We got to see him in a different way. We got to see him relaxed as a young man and growing into this incredible player. It was fun to see that; he just loved it. He would always talk about the things he was going to do and the places he was going to go.

I remember one time, when we were up in Banff [Alberta], at Banff Springs on kind of a mid-winter break during a West Coast swing, and the other flight attendant and I were going skiing. Now the guys aren't supposed to go skiing, because if they hurt themselves it could violate their contract. So they'd say, "No, we're not going skiing." Then wink-wink, nod-nod.

"So the other flight attendant and I are up on the mountain skiing, and all of a sudden we see some of the players—and Sergei was one of them. He was going balls out, straight down the mountain, with his hands up in the air, screaming, "I love America!" And one of his team-mates yells, "You big dummy. You're in Canada!"

Sergei just smiled and said, "Oh."

Playing the Trust Card

As coach and GM of the Red Wings when the Soviets began immi-grating to Detroit, Bryan Murray understood the delicate machi-nations it would take to get even a thoroughbred like Sergei Fedorov comfortably acclimated to his new environment. His long talks paid off years later when Murray was the GM in Anaheim and Fedorov, inexplicably to many, was looking for a new gig elsewhere.

According to Bryan Murray:

There were some early days when Sergei wasn't treated altogether fairly. I know he was in my office quite often as a young player, talking about not only on-ice stuff but off-ice as issues had come up. But he was a strong guy, and all we suggested to him was just to go play the game. Use what you can as far as your ability is concerned and you'll be fine. And obviously he was more than fine. He became a great player.

I think any young player, and in particular with a young player speaking a different language, it was an issue. His style of play was an issue. His newness to the NHL was an issue. It was my obligation, our responsibility as management and coaches, to deal with our players on an individual basis.

Sergei was a good guy. He really wanted to be good. He knew he could be. He was a ready listener and a good learner. And he became a very important player. We had a good relationship. And I remember many times, after I went elsewhere, getting the signal from Sergei to say hello.

As far as recruiting him to Anaheim, I'm not sure I had to talk very hard. The contract was just part of it. His importance to our team in Anaheim at that time was important to him. So I think role was a key factor. That and knowing each other helped. And knowing where we were trying to go with the team in Anaheim certainly helped.

Those are sometimes the kinds of issues you have to deal with when you're trying to recruit a player. And he came out there with us, even though he was an older player at that time, but he was a really good player for me.

I think he had great fun in Detroit. But I knew him and I think we could trust each other. I don't know this, but maybe Sergei just felt it was time to have a change and to try his ability elsewhere.

They're with the Band

On July 21, 1992, I drove into a crowded parking lot around the Pontiac Silverdome, pulled a little rank and slipped my car into a slot reserved for the media—for a three-act rock concert I was attending as a fan, certainly not as a music critic for my newspaper. Again, figuring I'd try to exert what little influence a media ID might allow me, one of the friendly security guys happened to be a Red Wings fans—and it just so happened his team was starting to create some real excitement around town.

So we talked a bit, and he was kind enough to advise me that, considering the crowd, we really didn't want to sit on the floor near the stage, as our tickets allowed. Instead, he ushered my wife and me to the press box, where I'd sat many times before on Sundays, and the occasional Thanksgiving Day, to help cover the hapless Lions for the Detroit Free Press.

It was about 9:30 p.m. One band had performed, and the second had just started its set. Guns N' Roses, the band we'd come to see, wouldn't get on the stage until 10 minutes before midnight. About halfway through the second act, I felt two big strong hands on my shoulders giving me a brief, deep massage. I turned to see Sergei Fedorov, beaming. He was with a small group that included

*Vladimir Konstantinov, and the security guys offered them safe
haven in the press box as well.*

*But as it turned out, Sergei and his group would find a better place
to enjoy and get to know the band in a long and unforgettable night.*

———————•——————————————•———————

Sergei Fedorov remembers, sort of:

Somehow, I don't remember exactly, we had become friends with the
manager of Guns N' Roses. We really enjoyed their music since day
one. Michael [Chovich], my interpreter and good friend, was playing
their songs on his guitar a little bit. Not like Slash or anything like that,
but when we were hanging out, he was trying to explain what Guns N'
Roses was.

Eventually, they were touring and stopped in Detroit: Faith No More,
Metallica, and Guns N' Roses, the last gig of that show. I don't know
how, but after the show we were backstage, and we were hanging out
with most of the band except Axl [Rose]. Axl was in a different room.
He came out to grab some champagne and shrimps, then went back to
that secluded room, I guess. That's how he behaved, so it was normal.

But we got to know that night most of the other guys. A couple of
them had a little knowledge about hockey, so we had a great time. We
were a little bit buzzed and tired, and when we got out of that football
arena there was one car left. It was ours. How cool is that?

It was amazing. It was a great time. We talked about it over the years
about Guns N' Roses and how cool that night was for us to join them,
take some pictures, and hang out with them. Good music. Good band.
Really world class.

A Thoroughbred
Among Clydesdales

*Sergei Fedorov is undisputedly one of the three greatest players
ever to wear a Red Wings sweater. He had as much raw talent as
Gordie Howe, and he could skate faster and handle the puck even
better than Steve Yzerman. But Fedorov confounded coaches, frustrated teammates, and baffled fans because, they said, they never
knew what he would bring to the ice from game to game. That
changed fairly quickly after Scotty Bowman arrived.*

●————————————————————————●

At least according to Dave Lewis:

Sergei was so talented, but he was also very misunderstood at times.
Every player goes through different levels of performance and Sergei's performance level, when he was on top of his game, was untouch-
able. He'd be unstoppable. But at times, when something was bother-
ing him, like any athlete, you don't always have your A game, and that
would affect him in a way that maybe his performance looked like he
didn't care.

That bothered some fans and media. But I think deep down Sergei
cared a lot about his performance. It's hard to always bring your A game.

And when he was on his B game, or his C game, he really got criticized. That might've bothered him maybe more than it should have.

Misunderstanding Sergei would be an easy thing to do. He was tremendous, and he didn't like not playing at the high level. He also didn't like not being used in those key situations. At times that bothered him, and that bothered his performance. Fans wanted this high, high level of performance all the time, which is impossible to do.

And when Scotty arrived, well, it took Sergei a lot longer to figure out Scotty than it took Scotty to figure out Sergei. And in dealing with Sergei—like all high-level athletes, Sergei was a thoroughbred—you just treat thoroughbreds differently than Clydesdales. There's a different mentality; there's a different mindset.

Scotty treated players differently than any coach I'd ever been around. He treated players by their stature in the game. And that's how he communicated with them. He would rarely call a player in and have a 10-minute conversation with him in his office. He would communicate to you by how you were used on the ice. If it was late in the game and we needed a big face-off win in the left corner, it was, "Kris Draper, you go and take the face-off." If we needed to score a power play goal, and we needed a net front guy, Scotty would say, "Tomas Holmstrom, you're going to be in the net front."

Scotty knew what type of player he needed for the team to be successful. And when I say successful, I mean win the Stanley Cup. That was one of his biggest strengths: He knew what it took to survive these wars, these battles, the grinding week after week of playoffs, and how to get to the Finals and win. He knew what type of people he needed.

Sergei eventually figured out Scotty. But Scotty knew what he wanted from Sergei and how to get it—maybe not directly one on one. Maybe he'd go to another player to have a talk with Sergei, like Igor [Larionov] or Slava [Fetisov].

And obviously Sergei grew under Scotty to be the player that he became, even playing on defense for about a month. That took everybody by surprise. Sergei probably didn't like playing defense, but he liked believing that Scotty had that much confidence in him that he could play him on defense, especially when Scotty would say, "You could win the Norris Trophy, Sergei, if you really applied yourself to defense."

I don't know if that was an experiment, but it was something that told Sergei, "I think that you're a really good player." And Scotty knew when to send those messages to him, not so much verbally, but through his actions on the bench. That was one of Scotty's greatest strengths.

Life with Scotty: 'An Intense Time'

Listen to Sergei Fedorov nearly two decades later talking about his coach and he sounds like he's still trying to figure out Scotty Bowman. While vastly different than the brutality with which Viktor Tikhonov dealt with players on the CSKA and the Soviet National Team, Bowman nevertheless found ways to ratchet up the discomfort level, keep his players constantly guessing, and raise their level of play while creating the kind of team chemistry that would take them to the summit.

Here's Sergei Fedorov's take:

From the Soviet Union to the NHL North American hockey—two very different survival systems. Viktor Tikhonov, he was hard on everybody, the different methods under his command. I can go on forever. Scotty was a little bit more tricky, more mental games. He wants you to understand why—and think about it. He's not going to prepare you every day like a babysitter. No, he will actually make you understand: if you want this one thing, to win the Stanley Cup, then you have to do this, plus double more than. Then you will be fine.

Scotty made you think and understand. He brought a new coaching style. He wanted us to do new stuff on the ice, play as a team more often. He wanted to add more players, better players, players who can play big games, big tournaments, big playoffs.

Eventually it's my take on Scotty later on, after many years, he was cool, just cool, relaxed. I didn't really see him a lot of times go out of his way and be mad at us. Later, after I finished my career in the NHL, I understood he knew what it was going to take to get us there, to win that first Cup, then the second Cup.

He knew it would be difficult, and he gave us speeches that we will never forget. You understood one thing only: If you want to do something like that, we have to become not a team but a family. We have to respect each other, our moods, our thoughts. We had quite an experienced team and everyone wanted ice time. That's where he became Scotty, in our mind.

It was hard to understand his moves at any one time. It was hard the first year or two, even three, to understand what was going on. Eventually, I understood that the simple things he wants from you are quality and the same level of intensity, and then he would play you forever. I figured that out after I didn't go on the power play for some time. Then he put me and Brendan [Shanahan] on PK [penalty killing]. I understood Scotty was not happy with our game.

So it was an intense time. It's hard to guess what's going on. Why is he doing it? Then we got used to it after a year or two. At that time we had a really smart group of players, a really hardworking group that can understand without talking too much what we want to achieve and how we want to go about our business.

Once we understood, it was a lot of fun to trick people. By the time they figured it out, we were already past that team in the playoffs.

Scotty already knew what was going to happen. And it worked. It really would.

I think I got it. I think it worked out for me and for the team—and for Scotty also.

For Fedorov, the Highest Praise

Brendan Shanahan was among the final pieces to the Stanley Cup roster, acquired in a blockbuster trade at the start of the 1996-97 season. (Hall of Fame defenseman Larry Murphy, another important piece, came at the trade deadline the following spring.) But it didn't take Shanahan long to appreciate the immense skills of No. 91.

———————•———————

Here's Brendan Shanahan:

Sergei is probably the most talented player I've ever played with, the most gifted naturally. As a player there was nothing he really couldn't do when he put his mind to it. He probably could've won a Norris Trophy as a defensemen if he'd decided to.

Sometimes Scotty would say, "Go shadow Mike Modano," and Sergei would just skate with him the whole game. Whatever Sergei wanted to do on the ice, he could. He was strong, so quick, and he had a great shot. Our power-play breakout, no matter what we drew up, we all sort of knew: give the puck to Sergei and get out of his way. Just let him carry it in and then we'll set up.

And what a fabulous person. I always thought before I knew Sergei that he was this sort of cool Hollywood guy. But he was actually this very sensitive, kind guy. Kind, almost in some ways, a childlike person, the way his approach to hockey was. He was like a kid. I think he just enjoyed being out on the ice and skating.

While some of us saw it as a business and a responsibility, Sergei just had fun playing.

The Russians
Were Better, Period

It didn't take Bryan Murray long to see the difference between North American and Soviet hockey. And he couldn't help but be impressed. The challenge, ultimately, for the Wings' coach and GM was how to meld them onto the roster in Detroit when the Russians started arriving in the early 1990s.

Here's Bryan Murray:

When I first saw the Russian Red Army come over and play, we didn't expect what they brought —the skill level and skating ability. They played a puck-possession type of game that we weren't used to seeing so often in the NHL. And then when players started to come over to the NHL, I understood: they were better.

They were better than a lot of our players. They held the puck longer. They wanted to play with the puck rather than chase it. And they were going to take jobs away from North American players. I understand some players in some organizations were worried that they were going to be out of the NHL when these Russian players and European players came over at that time. And they [Europeans] put up with some stuff too. But they brought an outstanding dimension to our game. They added to the NHL in many, many ways with their ability and skill level.

It was pretty easy to see that the Europeans, the Russians, were way ahead of us. You see the way we coach kids over here. We have one puck on the ice that they all fight over. The Europeans have 100 pucks, and they all skate. They did lots of skating, and when they skated, they had a puck on their sticks the entire time. They learned to pass, how to do things in tight little areas. The last time I was in Europe watching a Midget game, their puck skills were just unbelievable.

And you saw that with the Russian Five playing together. They were never afraid to regroup, because of their puck skills. They knew there weren't going to be many miscues. We play up-and-down hockey in North America. Our practices involved lots of shooting, maybe one pass, shoot the puck, hit somebody, and get the drill over with, then move on.

I really think the Russians in particular, when they came over here, they had such great puck-possession skills that it really changed our game. We loved what we saw. It opened all of our eyes. We saw how these guys were going to have a big impact on winning teams. The issue was how we were going to fit them onto our teams. That was a big moment for us, and the reason it worked was because we had Steve Yzerman. When we first brought the young Russians over, he was very open-minded. He was such a great captain. He recognized why they won. He saw what these guys were bringing to the Detroit Red Wings.

He really helped to integrate them. But the players themselves, the three younger Russians who first came over here, were such good guys too. If they hadn't been good guys, it would have been harder, for sure.

'What's the Number?'

Sergei Fedorov lived the American dream in a way most Americans cannot even imagine: Hollywood good looks, magnificent physical condition, with a bank account to ensure his every need and whim—a true 1-percenter in every way. Yet he never forgot who he was, what he was here for, and why it all mattered.

● ——————————————————— ●

Here's Dave Lewis:

Sergei came to North America and he had it all—freedom, some money—and he enjoyed the lifestyle. He enjoyed Detroit. When his family came over here, his mom and dad and his brother, Sergei really appreciated that. I think all his hard work, in Sergei's mind, had finally paid off.

He had played with some great players in Russia, but now he's in America on an NHL team that thinks highly of him. The fans think highly of him. The media love him. And he's got this certain flair about his game. He's one of the purest, best skaters I've ever seen. The fans recognized that right away.

He's got the long flowing hair, and he would pull up to the arena in a different car every three months. If it wasn't a Porsche, a Ferrari, or a Mercedes, then there was something wrong. He dressed impeccably. He was living the life, and he really enjoyed it. And I'm not saying he abused it.

One funny story I can tell you about Sergei coming to training camp every year: We always had these tests in the locker room, and one of these tests for about three or four years in a row was a pull-up contest. Some of these young college players who were drafted or maybe invited to the camp would train specifically for this test.

And so the record at this particular camp was something like 26, set by some guy you'd never heard of; I don't know who he was, a college kid, not a big guy. Well, Sergei would come in and say, "Okay, what's the number this year?" And the trainer would say, "It's 26 this year, Sergei." So he would get up on the pull-up bar and do 27, make it look easy, then quit. He wouldn't do 28 or 29; he'd do 27, then stop.

I'm just making the point that while he lived the lifestyle, he also trained and worked hard and took his job seriously. He always wanted and expected to be a top performer on the ice.

Burning from the Inside?

Few people knew Vladimir Konstantinov better than Slava Fetisov. Certainly no one knew him longer. Fetisov's brother, Anatoly, and Vladdie were teammates in youth hockey and good friends. Konstantinov would often wind up at the Fetisovs for a home-cooked meal, and soon Slava took him under his wing.

Here's Slava Fetisov:

Vladimir, he was kind of a wild kid, but always well-respected. They called him "Grandpa," even when he was 15 or 16, because he was so serious, so tough and gruff.

A few years later, he was my teammate, and he was still wild, thinking he could do everything by himself. For him, it was 100 percent a hockey life. He just said, "I will give it more than anything." He had a huge heart, but we were playing one game and I could see he was getting tired in the third period. I started to watch. I see that he is not drinking water. And I asked him why, and he said, "Because they told us not to drink."

But that was true in the Soviet system. We practice four times a day and they do not give us water. They say we burn from the inside, not to drink the water and you get faster in shape. It is kind of a crazy philosophy, but that is how it was.

He was great kid, always so funny, you know, telling Russian jokes, especially in dressing room. We lace the skates and he starts joking, some sarcastic stuff. He was so funny to be around. But on the ice, completely different. Very serious. He was so honest to the game. He played very moment at 120 percent.

That's Using Your Head, Eh?

They call it "the Punch-Up in Piestany," a brawl in Czecho-slovakia between bitter historical rivals that got so out of control that officials turned the lights out in hopes that the fighting would eventually end. And these were kids competing in the World Junior Championship in 1987. One guy was in the middle of it all, and he wound up being a teammate in Detroit with a guy from the other side who also was in the middle of it all—and made a bit of a name for himself with a headbutt that rearranged another guy's face. You shouldn't be surprised.

Brendan Shanahan remembers:

I was 17, and we were at the World Juniors. Interestingly, the format back then was round robin, so they took the two best teams from the previous year and they put them in the last game of the tournament. Canada was actually fighting for the gold medal, and we had to win the game, I think, by three or four goals maybe. And the Russian team, at the time they were USSR, the Soviet Union, they had a horrible tournament. They were a frustrated group. I think they were in fifth or sixth, so they were just playing it out.

We didn't know this at the time, but I found out later that they were embarrassed and they were being ridiculed by their coach. They sort of feared repercussions when they went back. They weren't being fed after games. It was a combustible moment. So what started out as some pushing and shoving on the ice turned into a couple of guys fighting, which turned into three or four guys fighting, and then it turned into a five-on-five brawl, which was unheard of at the time in international hockey.

It's funny, you know, players and people right now don't see bench-clearing brawls in hockey, but they did exist back then for us. Most of us were playing major or junior hockey. By then I had already been in three of them. There was a bit of a code as to how these things occurred. The rule was, you didn't go over the boards first, but if one team left the bench, *they* were in trouble and then you left the bench to make sure the numbers were even. The team that left the bench second or the individuals who left the bench second were exonerated. So during this five-on-five, all of a sudden, there was a fight down to our left and we were all watching the fight, somewhat in disbelief. But as 16-, 17-, 18-year-old kids, we were pretty excited. The Russian bench was to our right and two Russian players went by us to join the fight, making it seven on five.

Burt Templeton was our head coach, and in that moment he knew what we were going to do, and he realized that the repercussions would be different. I remember thinking that I was just going, and Luke Richardson thought he was just going, and probably a lot of our guys just thought, *Okay, we'll just send out a couple of guys to even the numbers out.* But as it turned out, we all went, and they all went, the Russians. And it was a wild and dirty fight.

As it turned out, we had some fighters on the Canadian team, some guys who were used to it. But we also had some guys like Pierre Turgeon and Glen Wesley who were not fighters. And you know when you had a bench-clearing brawl and your team went, everyone went, but there always were two or three guys on each team who would just grab onto each other, as non-fighters, and just hold on and kind of talk and admire what was going on.

But the Russians, they just assumed everyone goes, everyone fights, so we had some guys on our team who got beaten up pretty badly by some real strong guys. We didn't know who we were dealing with. You didn't know if you were paired up with Alexander Mogilny or if you were paired up with Vladimir Konstantinov, so it was a scary situation. It was a wild, wild brawl, and they eventually had to turn the lights out.

I thought at the time that they're turning the lights off because they want this to end. To me it was a signal to stop. "Let's just turn the lights out for a second here." But I've got to tell you, some things got done when the lights were out, and *that* was what ended the fight. When the lights came back on, there was a clear winner and there was a clear loser in each matchup, and that did sort of end things.

The referees had left the ice. It was something. I don't know that anybody could be prepared for something like that, let alone a bunch of kids. Burt Templeton, our coach, had torn his sport coat in two, I guess reaching to grab players as they were spilling over the boards.

I never saw the headbutt.

We all finally went into the dressing room, and some of our guys were pretty banged up. Greg Hawgood's nose was somewhere over here, and he said that one of the Russian players hit him with a headbutt. It wasn't until I went home and we watched the video that we really saw how massive this fight was. Patrick Roy had a younger brother on the team, Stefan Roy, and he had a perfect circle on his forehead. I remember in the dressing room he was screaming, like, "Where were you guys?" Then I watched the video afterward and there were two guys on him beating him up, and one of them kicked him right in the head.

And I also saw the fight that Hawgood was in with Konstantinov. But the part of the story that Hawgood left out was that when they weren't punching anymore, Konstantinov went to put his sweater back on the proper way. And when he did that, Hawgood sucker-punched Vladdie—not knowing then that Vladdie's nickname would someday be The Impaler. At that moment, Vladdie head-butted him right in the face—just dropped him to the ice with a broken nose.

Dr. Jekyll and Mr. Hyde?

Universally revered by his teammates, loathed by opponents, and admired by every coach who enjoyed winning hockey games, Vladimir Konstantinov seemed to inspire a story or two, or many, in everyone he encountered. Some describe him as though he were two different people, or one with a Dr. Jekyll and Mr. Hyde personality disorder—a terror on the ice, and something quite different, quite pleasant actually, away from the game.

●━━━━━━━━━━━━━━━━━━━●

Here's Igor Larionov:

Vladdie was actually, well, he was a tough sonofabitch, you know? He was a tough defenseman, playing kind of scrappy, always trying to be in your face. But when he was younger, he was playing center. He played forward in the 1986 World Championships in Moscow for the Soviet team. But when he played with the Red Army, he was a fourth-line guy, and it was hard for him to get in the lineup when we were kind of breaking in guys like [Sergei] Fedorov, [Pavel] Bure, and [Alexander] Mogilny.

It was tough in that system because the coach was harsh, always yelling and barking at the older guys, so you can imagine how much tougher it was on the younger guys. They're basically afraid, living on the edge, afraid to make mistakes or express themselves.

But you could see Vladdie's determination and character, so now he became a defenseman. Playing in North America, he because more physical. He could be in the face of anybody in the league. But he was actually doing really good defensively, and he also had some scoring ability, an offensive touch—like a piece of skill in his arsenal. And when Slava [Fetisov] came, Vladdie was able to do a lot more stuff because he was given more freedom to join the offense.

In the Red Army days, Vladdie was a quiet guy. When I saw him again in Detroit, when I got traded in '95, I could see that he was more mature. And he was playing for a good team. Already he was one of the top guys, along with Nick Lidstrom and Paul Coffey. But for me it was nice to see how Vladdie had become more solid, with more character—a guy you could rely on.

And once we started to play together [the Russian Five], his offensive abilities came to life again. He started to do a lot of stuff and he was enjoying the game, every minute of it. That year we won the Cup, I would say Vladdie started to play the best hockey of his life. There was no weaknesses to his game at that time. It was easy to see that he could play ten more years and dominate the league on defense.

In Russia, we used to call him *Dyed* [short for *Dyedushka*], which is like "Grandpa." He was grumpy, you know, always serious, never smiled, kind of like an old man. But his mentality, the soul inside him, he was a very gentle man, a very caring man.

Despite his toughness, his aggressiveness in the game, off the ice he was just a very, very good man.

'The Guy that
Every Team Feared'

It didn't take their Detroit teammates long to understand that the three younger Russians who joined the roster in the early 1990s were highly skilled hockey players who made their team a lot better. And for a guy who always played with a chip on his shoulder, patrolling Steve Yzerman's left wing like a fearsome barroom bouncer who took no prisoners, Gerard Gallant saw many of the same attributes in one special newcomer.

Here's Gerard Gallant:

Vladimir Konstantinov to me was the ultimate defenseman. He could do it all. He played a very tough game, a physical game. But he also had good puck skills. He could pass the puck; he joined the rush all the time. He was also a guy that every team feared because when you crossed the blue line he made you pay a price.

But what a great person. Vladdie had trouble with the English language and we always had fun talking with him. He would more or less grunt.

He always used to get mad at the other Russian players. He was a guy who came to work every day, and at practice sometimes when he'd see the other Russian players slack off a little bit, he was the guy who pushed them really hard. He didn't like that stuff.

Sergei Fedorov was the most talented player coming over. He was a young player. His speed at that time was unbelievable in this league. His talent level, some of the goals he scored were unbelievable too. They were all great hockey players by the time they got here.

After the first couple of years, nobody was saying this guy's not tough, or this guy doesn't play hard enough. Even [Slava] Kozlov, when he came over, he was a small guy but he battled and he was strong on every puck. They weren't fighters, but they were battlers and they played really hard.

Konstantinov was one of the toughest players I ever played with. He wasn't cheap, but he was dirty—and he backed it up. Sometimes you saw players who were dirty but didn't back it up. Not Vladdie. He hit hard, he played hard, and he always backed it up—not fighting-wise, but to play the game hard, battle, hit, and finish checks.

He definitely changed the way we thought of Russian hockey players.

'The Ultimate Warrior'

If there is such a thing as love at first sight between a coach and a hockey player, Bryan Murray experienced it when he first laid eyes on Vladimir Konstantinov. Murray was coach and general manager of the Red Wings, and Konstantinov was captain of the Soviet National Team at the 1991 World Championships in Finland. Nearly 25 years later, Murray had a vivid recollection of what he had witnessed.

Here's Bryan Murray:

My early impression was that this guy was just so competitive. He was running around hitting Canadians, Americans—whoever he was playing against. And every time he came to the bench, he took his sweater off and his shoulder pads. So obviously he had an injury of some sort. But he went back out and battled again, competed like crazy. And he had this big smile on his face any time he hit somebody.

So you just know that's a guy you want on your hockey team. He was the ultimate warrior, put it that way. And we're going to have this guy in Detroit if we can work a way to get him to come.

I remember meeting him out in the country in this wooded area.

We could tell that Vladimir looked at it as an opportunity to be an NHL player. But also, as he said through an interpreter, if we brought him out, arrangements had to be made for his family. That told me a lot about him.

What you saw on the ice from Vladimir Konstantinov was what you saw off the ice: a competitive, hardworking, honest guy willing to do whatever was necessary to be successful. And obviously it turned out really well for the Red Wings. After a short period of time getting to know him and coach him, I knew every time I put him on the ice that he was going to compete like heck.

Those types of players like Vladimir Konstantinov are rare. They never let you off the hook, even in practice. If you were competing against him, you had better compete hard, because he played on the edge all the time. Hard, and a little bit rough. And definitely dirty. I know as a coach and a manager that he's a guy you hate to play against because you have to battle every inch of the ice to get to the net.

Vladimir was a candidate for the Norris Trophy. I'm not sure why you get into the Hall of Fame and why you don't, but he probably would have gotten there with his ability to win. To be one of the top defensemen in the league, if not *the* top defenseman in the league at that time, probably would have allowed him the chance of getting in. That's why it's sad that it was cut so short.

Even Teammates Weren't Safe

You know by now that for Vladimir Konstantinov there was only one way to play the game—even in practice. And it often led to confrontations with his own teammates.

Here's Kris Draper:

Vladdie was a guy who, no matter if it was practice or Game 7 of the Stanley Cup Finals, you're getting the same effort. I mean, he ran us in practice. We couldn't quite understand why he would do that to his own teammates. Sometimes you'd think he didn't like you the way he would practice against you, but that's what made Vladdie one of the fiercest competitors I ever played with.

You watch the battles that he had, probably the early impression that I had of him, with Jeremy Roenick of the Chicago Blackhawks. Those guys just went at it; it was amazing to watch. And when you're sitting there on the bench, a teammate of Vladimir Konstantinov, and you see the way he plays and you see the way he competes, it's contagious. You can't wait to get over the boards; you want to compete at that level. Vladdie just made players around him better.

He was basically built out of the same mold as Chris Chelios. We had epic battles with Chris when he was with the Chicago Blackhawks. But that's the guy, when you're going into battle and you're playing in a big game, you want in your locker room—the Vladimir Konstantinovs. Similar to how it was with Chris Chelios. That's how I kind of compare what Vladdie was going to be, how good he was going to be.

Like a DC Comic Hero— or Villain

Clark Kent was a mild-mannered reporter in Gotham City, but when he saw trouble he ducked into a phone booth for a quick change and became Superman, then made life miserable for the bad guys. Vladimir Konstantinov was an equally mild-mannered husband and father, but when he went into a locker room to change out of his Armani suits into a Detroit Red Wings uniform, he wreaked his own brand of havoc on the perps from the other team.

Dave Lewis admired it on a nightly basis:

If you watched Vladimir Konstantinov walk into a rink after getting off a bus, you would probably have thought he was not a regular player. He might have been an extra guy or maybe a seventh defenseman. But once he put the skates on and pulled a jersey over his head and stepped on the ice, you knew this guy was a warrior. He was fearless.

You don't see that in street clothes. The only place you can really identify a hockey player is in the game, on the ice, because there's no place to hide. You can't hide your character. You can't hide your skill. You can't hide your focus. You can't hide your determination. You can't do that because you're performing against players of the same level. When Vladdie slipped his jersey on, he became . . . it was almost like—I don't know—a Batman character.

And off the ice he became this humble, quiet, meek, and unassuming guy who wouldn't say much and didn't require any maintenance. "Maintenance" is a word you use as a coach. He was a low-maintenance player. He didn't require the accolades, the fans, the interviews. He never talked about his game. It was always about something else, somebody else. And he was very humble.

The biggest things about him that we saw were on the ice. The other teams would viciously attack him, thinking that would change his game, change his style of play. And for me, to see him react the way he did was special because, if anything, it enlightened him to be even more of a difficult player to play against. I'm sure coaches told their players to make sure you make this guy pay because he's going to quit. Well, that was the last thing . . . I don't even know if Vladimir Konstantinov knows what the word "quit" is. That's the type of personality that he was, that he still is!

Fans in Detroit love a player that won't back down. Vladdie would get knocked down, but he'd get right back up. And it didn't matter who it was against. It could be a fighter. It could be the most skilled guy on the team. It could be the biggest guy on the team. That's what the fans saw in Vladdie that they appreciated. You know they were thinking, *I would love to be that person, never back down in any situation.*

He also played injured, and his teammates admired him for that. He was rugged. He trained hard. The fans had so much respect for all the Russian guys. They tried to help them whenever they saw them. I saw that at official functions with fans. They couldn't get enough of the Russians. They wanted to be close to them. They wanted to talk to them.

They wanted to understand what made them tick: Why did they come? Why do they love Detroit so much? That's what I saw.

I don't know much about the hardships, but the courage it took to leave the Soviet Union and come to the United States was something that he brought to the game every night, just something he had in him. I don't know how you teach courage. I think it's impossible. You either have it or you don't. But somewhere growing up he developed this fearlessness.

I think that helped his transition, emotionally and mentally, to leave knowing probably good things were to follow. He had to leave an environment that was not good, not the way he wanted, to become a better person and a better player. You saw that courage every time he stepped on the ice.

And what a comfort level for a coach. I used to joke that I just had to leave the door open and Lidstrom and Konstantinov were on the ice—if not together, then the other one was coming. It was great to have that ability to know what you're going to get as a coach every shift, game in, game out, regardless of the level of game. And the bigger the game, the better the performance Vladdie would have.

He played on the edge, and that's hard to do as a player, always on the edge of a penalty. And he was the smartest guy. He and Chris Chelios were the smartest defensemen I know who knew that edge. Vladdie learned that young, or he picked it up somewhere along the way. But he knew how to play on that edge.

The year he had when we won, that particular season, it was like the light got brighter for him. He got to see everything clearer, everything was more crisp in his game, his performance, how his teammates supported him, how he played against his opponents. I think he really got it that year, what he could actually do—not just some of the time, but all the time.

As a young player coming into the league, you try to establish yourself. Survival at first is No. 1. Then you grow as a player. Vladdie took it to another level where the wheels started to turn a little bit more. He became not just a good player sometimes but a good player all the time. He started to put numbers on the board. He started to play against the other teams' best players all the time—and be effective. He got international recognition from the media. He got people identifying him as a Norris Trophy candidate. He never said anything about it, but you could see the confidence in his eyes on a nightly basis.

After he started getting that media attention, once people started to recognize his abilities, locally, nationally, and internationally, it didn't change him at all. Then he just knew that maybe people appreciated what he brought to the table every night. And that would be the only gratification he got out of it. He never really asked for recognition, but people finally identified who this guy was, what he was made of, what kind of player he was, and how it influenced the Detroit Red Wings.

One thing I learned about him: oh boy, he was good with kids. I had a couple of hockey camps that he came to and he would spend time with the kids. His language wasn't great, but he would smile and try to play some jokes on them. He was just a normal person. If you saw him sitting in a chair back then, he would be a normal guy just enjoying the sunshine of the day, or whatever.

He would come to my fantasy camps. I used to have these adult fantasy camps, five-day skating programs, three hours of ice each evening. They ended with a game for Make-A-Wish. And Vladimir Konstantinov would always come, free of charge, and he would sit in the locker room and get dressed with the players.

Some guys would be 30 years old; some guys would be 60 years old. Beer-league kind of guys. One guy was a doctor. One was an executive. One was a carpenter. They came to the camp and Vladdie would sit with them like he was one of them. He didn't feel like he was special. He didn't need another locker room to get changed in. He'd rub shoulders with them. They came from all over Canada and the U.S.—one came from London, England—and they couldn't believe that this was Vladimir Konstantinov, the warrior on the ice who was so quiet and unassuming, sitting on the bench with them.

Yet Vladdie was just being a hockey player, like they were. And did they ever appreciate that. That was the thing about Vladdie: he just gave. He didn't think about it; it was just him—humble and kind. He knew that the game that week was for kids with cancer, Make-A-Wish, so he would sign autographs for the kids and sign all that stuff for these hockey players.

Just this quiet, ordinary guy—and he's a professional athlete at the peak of his career coming several nights that week for this stupid old Dave Lewis Fantasy Camp thing, you know? That's Vladimir Konstantinov.

The Impaler— on Figure Skates?

The one thing hockey people notice that most casual observers in the stands and the press boxes overlook is skating ability. We tend to forget that all these marvelous things the players are doing, from puck-handling, passing and shooting to bodychecking and fighting, they do on skates with blades that are about 20 inches long and less than 3/16 of an inch in width. On his blades, Vladimir Konstantinov was a virtuoso.

Steve Yzerman says so:

Vladdie was a unique defensemen. He was a true skater, a fabulous skater. He could have been a figure skater with his ability on his edges—backward, forward, and his lateral movement was sensational with his ability to hit and to take a hit.

And then he'd come up with these unbelievable goals where he would be playing with the other Russian players and they'd be whipping the puck around, and all of a sudden Vladdie had this ability to just disappear on a breakaway. He'd find a seam and Slava [Fetisov] or one of the guys, Igor, would find him with a pass and he'd just go. He had that little forehand-backhand move and score. And we'd all just be sitting on the bench, shaking our heads.

With him and Slava, Nick [Lidstrom] and Murph [Larry Murphy], we had a tremendously gifted offensive defense. But Vladdie was also one of those defensemen, like Scott Stevens or Denis Potvin prior to that, guys where, when they were on the ice and you were coming through the neutral zone, if you weren't aware they were on the ice, they were going to step up and hit you. That forced you to be extra careful, maybe delay a second. And that's huge. You had to always know where Vladdie was, and that had a tremendous impact on the game.

That team at that time in '96-97, we had a lot of very popular personalities, different personalities but popular guys around the hockey world. Obviously here around Detroit with Vladdie—you know Detroit loves the ruggedness, the hard-nosed play. He just went in there and he got hit hard and he hit hard and he had no fear. But they also appreciated his skills.

He might have been the most popular player on the team. And as his teammates, we had to love this guy—as a player and as a person. But his popularity among the fans was pretty special, particularly after that '97 playoffs when he was spectacular. The outpouring of affection from the fans wasn't a surprise for us at all. And he was coming into his own as a hockey player, an elite defenseman, and in Detroit fans recognized how really good he was and what a really unique player he was.

My first impression of Vladdie was that he was very quiet. He came to the rink and was always very professional, probably a little bit more outgoing than, say, Slava [Kozlov]. But he really kept to himself, very private. And he worked really hard, just another great natural athlete.

I'm not sure how much training in the off-season he did. I know he liked to play tennis and other sports. But he was always one of the fittest guys on the team when we did our testing at the start of the year.

Very professional. Zero maintenance other than injuries, and he'd play through any injury.

He never said a whole lot, but I believe he knew more English than he let on. He sure knew all the swear words and wasn't afraid to use them. He had a quick sense of humor. You could say something to him and he'd just whip back a response. Very witty, and the guys loved him for the way he was: a really unique guy, outgoing in kind of an introverted way, if that makes any sense.

And he never took himself too seriously. Mostly he came and he played, and then he went home and did his thing with his family.

The Next Wayne Gretzky?

When Slava Kozlov came to Detroit, he was a shell of his former hockey-playing self. Once the brightest young star in the Red Army galaxy—after a spate of defections and controversial departures—he arrived still showing the aftereffects of a horrific car crash that killed his teammate, the passenger in the vehicle Kozlov was driving on the way to practice.

In his early days around the Wings' dressing room, Kozlov said very little, staying mostly to himself. Perhaps that's how he acquired the nickname "Grumpy." And perhaps, when he figured out what it meant, he tended to cultivate it a bit. The thing is, I never saw that side of Slava Kozlov, and neither did some others who invested a little time getting to know this kind, gentle soul—who also had a bit of a dirty mean streak on the ice.

Once a prospect that GM Jimmy Devellano compared favorably to Wayne Gretzky, Kozlov's career was very much in jeopardy following the accident. Soviet military doctors had advised Kozlov's Red Army team that vision problems would likely end his playing days. Of course, those doctors may or may not have been influenced by a few of Mike Ilitch's American greenbacks.

*Until the accident, Kozlov had no intention of coming to Detroit.
After losing so many players, the Red Army Club started to pay its
stars fairly competitive wages, and Kozlov was getting paid more
money than he'd ever dreamed to play professional hockey just a
few miles from where he grew up—until the Red Army stopped
paying him while he was lying for weeks in a hospital bed. That's
when the Wings came to the rescue.*

●————————————————————●

Bryan Murray shares some impressions:

My first meeting with Slava Kozlov was after seeing him play in
Europe. He was this young, good-looking guy, a great talent. And
I remember coming home from that tournament and Nick [Polano] and
I, and Jimmy Lites and Ken Holland, we were all talking about him.

Then he had that car accident, and as he was lying in that hospital
bed in Moscow, Mr. Ilitch told Nick to go over and try to meet the medical people, the Red Army people, try to help out his family as much
as we could and encourage Slava to come over here and see some of
our doctors.

But when he came over, he looked like he had just gotten out of
his sick bed. His face was still damaged, disfigured a little bit. It was a
hard thing to overcome. He was frail-looking, smaller. Strength-wise, he
wasn't where he needed to be.

Maybe we should have put him in the minors and let him play there
a little bit, but he had a big heart, and after a few weeks he was in a hurry
to play in the NHL. At that time we were in a hurry to build a team too.

I remember the first game we played in St. Louis, and he had the puck the whole game. I said to a couple of guys, "We have the next Wayne Gretzky here! This guy might be a dynamic player in the NHL," which he turned out to be; it just took him a little while.

But there was no doubt about his skills. He came up with clutch plays, clutch goals. He had talent. He had skill. He could hold onto the puck. He was patient. He was also a great guy. I don't know if anybody was going to be another Wayne Gretzky, point-wise, but Slava Kozlov sure had the ability to get points. And at the end of the day he found a real nice niche in the NHL.

'A Very, Very Clutch Hockey Player'

Nobody joked more about Slava Kozlov's cranky personality than the guys who sat closest to him in the locker room, guys like Darren McCarty and Kris Draper. They laughed it off, like the rest of their teammates, but from the bench, they saw a special hockey player, one with a flair for the biggest moments in a hockey game.

●————————————————●

Here's Kris Draper:

I always loved to tease Slava. He was probably as grumpy as any guy I've met. He's the same age as me, and I couldn't quite understand it. Here I am, walking into the same rink as he is, and I'm just thrilled to be in the NHL. I'm thrilled to be a Red Wing. But that's Kozzie.

Then all of a sudden the puck drops and—I'd have to say that out of all the Russian Five, Kozzie got overlooked considering what he did and how he played. Everyone would talk about the playmaking of Igor Larionov or the speed of Sergei Fedorov or the grit of Vladdie Konstantinov, and not a lot of [praise] went to Slava Kozlov.

But I tell you, you watch game film and you watch the goals that he scored, Slava Kozlov was a very, very clutch hockey player for the

Detroit Red Wings. He scored some big goals for us. He just had a really quick release and a good shot. And he was a very good complementary player. He was a great hockey player no matter who he was playing with.

19 Going on 16

Few people outside his family and his four Russian teammates knew and understood Slava Kozlov better than Jim Lites, who helped to bring him to Detroit and later tried to sign him with the Dallas Stars when Kozlov was a free agent playing in Atlanta. And their relationship has long transcended the sport of hockey.

Here's Jim Lites:

Slava Kozlov is my friend. I was probably closer to him as just a guy than a hockey player. He was represented by my younger brother [Scott Lites] as a player agent. They're still friends. And Slava and I have gotten together post-career. We've stayed in touch. He's a guy I can relate to. I have so much respect for him, and I really like him.

My perception of him from the beginning was that he just seemed pretty human to me. The other [Russians], when they came over here, were 19 to 20 going on 25. The Russian system pushed them in that direction. Slava, he was 19 going on 16 when I first met him. He wasn't able to let go emotionally when we tried to bring him over the first time. He didn't want to leave his mom. He didn't want me to pressure him to leave.

Then he had that bad accident, and to this day, whenever I have any contact with Slava, he's very appreciative for everything we were able to do for him and for having the opportunity to play in Detroit.

I know he was resentful of being traded out of Detroit. He got traded to Buffalo [in the deal for Dominik Hasek], and he hated [Coach] Lindy Ruff. They never hit it off. He loved being in Detroit. He loved being affiliated with the other Russians. It meant a lot to Slava. And he was the least affected of the bunch.

He had a great career in Detroit. Who scored more important goals in playoff games than Slava Kozlov? He was an unbelievable money player. This guy scored goals that other guys didn't—and couldn't. And somehow, he was the least heralded guy of the bunch. I just like the guy.

Cradle of Creativity

The hockey-crazed community of Voskresensk is awfully proud, and rightly so, of its tradition of developing some of the most dynamic and successful hockey players in the world. Here's one talking about another: a lifelong neighbor down the road, and a teammate in Detroit—check that: Stanley Cup champions in Detroit.

Here's Igor Larionov:

S lava Kozlov was born and raised in my hometown, Voskresensk. And according to our long hockey tradition, he was influenced by the famous Soviet coach Nikolai Epstein. Kozzie's father [Anatoly] played for Khimik, the team in the top league, and he coached me for a couple of years when I played for the top team.

As Kozzie grew up, he knew the style of the game from the famous Voskresensk hockey school, which was known for [developing] creative players. So when I got to Detroit, it was easy for me to figure him out as a player because I knew him. And he was actually pleased when he could pass somebody the puck and then get it back. That's what Kozzie was looking for.

He wanted to score goals, but he wanted to score them in a certain way. He was a good asset to play without the puck, to get in open space. He knew that the puck was always going to be there for him. And you know, he scored a lot of big goals for us.

No 'Average Joe'

The Red Wings annually enjoyed short summers in the Russian Five heyday—long playoff runs that butted up against the summer solstice, then training camp the second week of September, latest. But they made the most of those summers, whether or not they were parading the Stanley Cup around. One lovely afternoon, assistant coach Dave Lewis took his kids, Ryan and Megan, to visit the Kozlov's waterfront home to enjoy some water skiing.

Ryan took one of Kozlov's wave-runners for a little spin and got a ticket for speeding in a no-wake zone. That's about the most Slava Kozlov could ever be accused of making waves—and he was watching from shore. Kozlov wound up paying the ticket. It cost him a hundred bucks.

●━━━━━━━━━━━━━━━●

Here's Dave Lewis:

Slava Kozlov came to the Red Wings a few years after Sergei [Fedorov] had gotten there, and by then the dynamics in the locker room had changed. When Sergei got there, there was still some resentment, some understated comments that we don't want Russians taking our jobs.

By the time Slava came, things had changed a little bit. We had some younger players, some different players, and it was easier for Kozzie to be accepted. The other players, they understood that if new guys coming in could help them on the ice, it didn't take long for that acceptance to take place. That helped.

But, yeah, there was still this perception that you couldn't win a Stanley Cup with Russians. The focus was on those guys [Russians] until it was proven that it could be done. And they [again, the Russians] felt it was unfair because they gave their all every game; from training camp on, every performance was from the heart—like all our guys.

They felt no differently when we won or lost than any teammate, whether it was Steve Yzerman, Darren McCarty, or Kris Draper, but they felt they were harshly criticized when we lost because they were Russians. And these guys played for their Olympic teams, for their national teams. That had some skewed effect on some of the media.

Slava Kozlov was a real character guy, a quiet guy. Very professional, very serious, he trained hard. He would go early in practice to do special drills just to improve his game. He was sort of the forgotten one of the five, but he had a very strong influence on the team and on the success of the Russian Five.

I remember seeing him running the Joe Louis Arena stairs, up and down, as training. I think he might still have the record for doing that, in terms of all the athletes who have gone through the Red Wings organization. He was explosive and fast, but the biggest difference between Slava Kozlov and Sergei Fedorov was how the spotlight followed Sergei all around and Kozlov was in the shadow.

But he preferred that. He didn't want to be the front-and-center guy. He just wanted to be the guy his teammates respected, the guy fans could appreciate. He was highly skilled, very determined. He was also a private, unassuming individual who enjoyed just being himself and being in small groups.

Away from the rink, he kept to himself. He wasn't flashy. I think he appreciated being in North America. He appreciated the freedoms and lifestyles. But he didn't broadcast it. He just wanted to be Joe Average, but when it came to the rink, he became an athlete. That's what Kozzie was: very unassuming, always low maintenance. You didn't have to motivate him. You didn't have to tell him much for him to perform, and the coaches appreciated that.

Slava Kozlov,
in His Own Words

Whoever offered the advice to speak softly and carry a big stick could have had Slava Kozlov in mind. He is a man of few words, in any language—in his native Russian, and certainly in English, the language he resisted learning throughout his dazzling 17-year North American hockey career, including nine years in Detroit.

But while he may not be a storyteller like some of his celebrated Red Wings teammates, he never ducked a question. And though he may have been "a grumpy bastard" to many of his teammates, I always found him to be polite, kind, and generous with his time. He invited me not once but twice to his home in Voskresensk, sub-urban Moscow's City of Champions, introducing me to his parents and his grandfather and showing me around the beautiful little rink, the Podmoskovie Sports Palace, that stands as a cathedral/ museum near the city's center.

Kozlov is back home in Russia now, coaching in the Kontinental Hockey League. We interviewed him when he was an assistant coach of HC Spartak.

What follows is a lightly edited, condensed, and translated version

*of an interview that lasted nearly two hours and was conducted
in Russian.*

What do you remember about the first game the five of you played together?

Right off the bat, we clicked. The last player we got was Igor Larionov. From the very first training session and the very first game, we started scoring. We really started enjoying it; that is how I felt. I really enjoyed it. Before Igor, of course, we played with [Slava] Fetisov, [Sergei] Fedorov, and [Vladimir] Konstantinov, but once Igor got there everything kind of fell into place. And the hockey that we started playing, North Americans did not understand. They didn't know how to play against us.

What did it feel like, being part of that famous group?

I was the youngest one, and I just wanted to play. I did not think about it; I did not think which hockey style we were playing or who we were playing. I just came out and enjoyed playing hockey. I got a lot of advice from the older guys, and I learned a lot from them. When I was young I used to watch them on TV, how they played, [Vladimir] Krutov, Larionov and [Sergei] Makarov, Fetisov and [Alexei] Kasatonov—the Five. They made Russian and Soviet hockey infamous, and to be with such partners on the same line in Detroit, I got really, really lucky.

Of course I was proud that the Russians came and were playing as the Russian Five. It was even more prestigious for me to be a part of that five. I was just so happy that I was there, to be a part of that.

How did things change when Scotty Bowman joined the team?

Scotty Bowman came with his own vision. I did not know what to expect, what he was going to expect. The guys really helped me. I did not understand English, so they were translating for me. In time, it took Scotty 2 to 3 years to understand who he was going to keep, who was he going to trade. You have to give it to Scotty, he had a very special vision on how to create a team.

Slava came from New Jersey, and he was not very young. Igor came from San Jose. Scotty saw that by putting the Russian Five together, they could do something very original and groundbreaking—and turn hockey upside down in the NHL.

What were your impressions when you first joined the Red Wings, acclimating to life in the United States?

I did not pay attention to the little stuff. I just wanted to be a part of the team as soon as possible. I liked that I could go and get any hockey stick I wanted, gloves, skates, everything. After playing in the Soviet Union, it was unreal to go and have access to all this equipment. I could not believe it. You could order your own stick with a special curve, anything you wanted.

As a 15-year-old, you played in a tournament in Lake Placid with your Soviet teammates but without your name on the back of your sweater. Jim Devellano thought you were the best player on the ice, by far, and he thought your country was playing some kind of game by not identifying you at the time. Was that the case?

We did not have the best finances all the time, so we could not afford to write the names for everybody. I do not remember for sure about Lake Placid, but most likely that is what happened.

How were you guys treated by your teammates in the dressing room?

Everybody treated us with respect in the locker room. I had a really great relationship with everybody. I was next to Kris Draper and McCarty. I was the most closed off, I think, of all of us. I did not talk much to anybody, but my memories are extremely warm. And the guys treated us with big respect and understanding.

What are some of your favorite memories of that first Stanley Cup championship?

Game 4. We were really thinking that we wanted to finish the series in Detroit. The coaches were warning us that to lose one game at home and have to go back to Philadelphia, you do not know what would happen. I remember the night before, I could not fall asleep. I just kept thinking about that fourth game. In the morning I woke up; we were in the Greektown Hotel. We were getting ready in the morning and the whole team understood how important it was to win this Stanley Cup in Detroit.

So much pressure on you guys, such high expectations. What were those final seconds like when you knew you were finally going to win the Cup?

The atmosphere was out of this world. A lot of whistles at the end; the time was just going so, so slowly. I was sure we were not going to lose. That team was so amazing and so great; I think everybody felt that we were almost there. And the fans were great; they were really supporting us. I think that night there was no way we could lose.

And then you were a Stanley Cup champion. How did that feel?

It is a very unique feeling: that it is all over and that you finally won the Stanley Cup. The number of years that the team was going toward it, anything could have happened. You could have been traded; you could have gotten an injury. For me it was everything that I happened to be in the team that needed it and with the people who needed it. And finally the team won the Stanley Cup. It was a really unique feeling, and really warm memories.

What are your favorite memories of the celebrations that followed?

We had a lot of celebrations. The best was the parade. There were a lot of people there. I have never seen anything like that in my life. For me, everything was like a strange wonder. The fans of Detroit understand and love hockey, and they treated us, the Russians, with huge respect. And no matter if we won or lost, I never heard the fans say anything bad. They always supported us, no matter what.

And then you took the Stanley Cup for its first visit to Russia. What was that like?

I did not know Slava had problems asking the league for permission. I was just told that we were going with the Cup to Russia, and they gave me the schedule. Everything was greatly organized. Slava took the Cup to CSKA [Central Red Army Club] and a lot of young hockey players saw it. They saw the Stanley Cup. Igor, Slava, and I took the Cup to Voskresensk, Igor's and my hometown. My whole family was there, my nephew. It was great. For 3 to 4 days, we did not even sleep.

What do you think the Russian Five did for hockey both in Russia and in the United States?

Of course the Americans liked the game of the Russian Five, and they loved us. It probably gave an impulse for the relationship between the Americans and the Russians. But I don't know. At that time I didn't think about it; I just wanted to play hockey and enjoy the atmosphere. Every training session and every game with the Russian Five was the best school I ever went to.

What did the NHL experience with your group, and what did you learn from North American hockey?

What they found out about Russians is that the Russians know how to play hockey, that we are really good. And we learned from them too. We showed them combination hockey; they showed us physical hockey.

Many people describe you as the most underrated of the Russian Five. How did that make you feel?

I am very calm about it, and I think my purpose and my role were to not get in the way of the other players. I played with great partners, and right off the bat it started happening for me because of them. They were all much better than me. I knew it, and I accepted it, and I am very calm about it. I am just very proud that I won two Cups with them, and I am just extremely proud that I played in the same five with them.

You're a coach now. Do your players have any idea how famous you are?

I do not really talk about it. I do not tell people about it. Hockey is a team sport, so everybody won it together. Maybe they know. I won them as a player, and of course I would love to win them as a coach. But unlike a player, I cannot win anything anymore. I am just starting my coaching career, but I would love to win something as a coach someday.

You may have been underrated in hockey circles, but to people who watch The Simpson's on TV you're the most famous of all the Russian Five. How did that make you feel?

That is really funny. I guess that is how the Americans appreciated my game. Thank God, I got into somewhere. I guess I was not good enough for the Hall of Fame, but I got into the cartoon.

After so many great years, you returned to Russia, finished your career as a player, and then started a new career as a coach. How did that come about?

I came back here to play hockey, and after that I moved into the coaching position. The reason I became a coach is that I promised my father that I will try one day when I am done playing. My father was my coach, and I want to keep my promise to him. So I start to coach, and so far I'm really enjoying it.

Final thoughts, Slava?

Silence. A sardonic smile. A half-shrug.

Fade to black . . .

As the technicians were tearing down the set, Slava approached one of the producers and actually apologized for not being more helpful. He said he'd understand completely if his entire interview wound up on the cutting room floor. He could not have been more wrong, of course. But, seriously, how can you not love this guy?

Treated 'Like Meat'

To the most successful coaches, players are like chess pieces. Most of them are pawns, but some have special or unique skills, like the bishop, the knight, and the rook. It's how coaches deploy them that determines the outcome of games, of seasons, of Stanley Cup playoff tournaments. And in hockey circles Scotty Bowman is the undisputed grandmaster.

The men who played for him frequently didn't much care for his tactics, but they certainly appreciated his results. The people he worked for didn't much care for his tactics either, but they too loved his results. As a reporter who covered his team for years, I often despised his tactics—but I am not too proud to acknowledge that on virtually a daily basis he forced me to work harder. As a result, I got better at my job. And in the process, I had the privilege of covering a championship team. So, yeah, I get where his players are coming from.

Jim Lites was still in Detroit when Bowman was hired, a move that ended a bitter and divisive feud with his father-in-law, Mike Ilitch, who wanted to hire Mike Keenan as coach and GM to replace Bryan Murray. (Keenan wanted Jim Devellano out of the way too, as a matter of fact.) Soon after, Lites left the Wings

*for the franchise now based in Dallas, where he continues to hear
and cherish stories about the man who has Stanley Cup rings for
every finger and thumb on both hands—with four rings left over.*

———————————

Here's Jim Lites:

One of my absolute favorite characters ever. If I don't hear a story
every month from someone about Scotty Bowman, what he's done,
what he's accomplished or how just he is, how he coached, it wouldn't
be a good month. He has had a huge impact on our sport.

I can tell you that one of my best experiences in Dallas was working
with [former Stars GM] Bob Gainey, who won five consecutive Stanley Cups captaining Scotty Bowman's teams in Montreal. And the first
time I met Bob, I asked him about Scotty. He said, "I respect the guy
completely, and I hated playing for him. He'd use any deception possible to be successful. He'd lie to your face. He'd make you miserable.
When I was young, he treated me like meat. But he's a great coach and
I learned a lot from him."

That story goes on and on and on. Jim Nill [former Wings assistant
GM under Lites] just told me a story about Scotty Bowman and had us
all on the floor laughing. He's an amazing guy, Scotty. I saw him recently
at a Hall of Fame induction and saw how the man has unbelievable
energy for his age.

He's a genius—the greatest hockey coach in history.

'No Hard Feelings, Guys'

No one in the Detroit Red Wings' locker room better personified the dramatic change Coach Scotty Bowman brought to the team as soon as he arrived than his captain, Steve Yzerman. It didn't work overnight. It took him a few years to retool his roster to rid the players he didn't want in favor of those he knew he needed to win. Eventually it became a single-minded focus that carried them to the summit—and no one appreciated that more than the man who endured so many post-season heartbreaks.

Here's Steve Yzerman:

Scotty came in with a great pedigree of winning multiple Stanley Cups. And what he did with our team—it was a transition, or an evolution, from when Bryan Murray took over in 1990. Bryan put together a really skilled group. We were a really good team. Our team that lost to Toronto in '93 [first round, Game 7 loss in overtime], that was a really good team. Tremendous talent. We scored goals.

But what we needed over time was to improve defensively, to be able to win 1-0 games, 2-1 games. Those are the kind of games you have in the playoffs.

And Scotty just took that skilled team and added the defensive part. He demanded it. That ultimately took us from being a very skilled high-scoring team to one that could play defense too. We improved our overall play. We changed our mindset from "We're going to outscore you tonight" or "We've got to outscore you to win" to "We're not going to just outscore you; we're going to shut you down."

Instead of us making the mistake and the other team scoring the winning goal, we played to make sure they made the mistake. That was the evolution. Bryan had assembled a very skilled, talented group that could score. Scotty took that next step to mold it into a better defensive team, to get us over the hump.

With Scotty's influence, it became all about winning. Everything had to be about winning. He left us alone in the locker room. He came in and did his presentations and prepared us for practice, prepared us for games. But otherwise he left us alone. So the culture that he instilled was "No hard feelings here, guys, but this is all about winning. I'm not doing anything to hurt your feelings. It's not a personal thing. But we're going to win. This is what you need to do to win, and that's the way it is."

All of our guys bought into that. It proved to be correct, and we were successful. We really appreciated Scotty for that.

On Winning That Trophy

When Scotty Bowman speaks, we should all be paying attention.
So listen up and believe him when he talks about how truly diffi-
cult it is to win that big, beautiful trophy.

Here's Scotty Bowman:

It's always been hard, but it's much more difficult now with the parity.
It's a two-month marathon for sure, and injuries play a big factor. I
could go back to teams I was with, we thought we could win it and then
all of a sudden you're not healthy . . . And you have to have good goaltending; it doesn't have to be great, but it can't cost you in the playoffs.
We won with three different goalies when I was there in Detroit, which
is really unique.

You also have to have some experience. It's hard for young teams to
win Stanley Cups. You need some experienced players who have been
through it because you have to be ready to play at a higher level for two
months—and it's at the end of the season, not the beginning.

I think the Stanley Cup is the greatest trophy in sports, and it's probably the most difficult trophy to win, because you have to win 16 games.
And each round that you play, you have to elevate your game—three

times in a row because the team you're playing has just won a series. They're not maybe as good as you are, but they're better than the team you just beat.

That's where you have to have depth in the players you really depend on. You can check through the record books and see that role players mean an awful lot in the playoffs. Your go-to guys can't have bad games or bad series, but your depth plays a big part because you're playing every second night for two months—in the high 20s in the number of games. That's quite a lot of hockey with travel and everything else.

So there are a lot of things involved: goaltending, experience, depth, you have to stay healthy. And it doesn't hurt to be a little fortunate too.

Bowman Finally Gets His Man

Long before he finally made his NHL debut in 1989 with the New Jersey Devils, even before, as a young defenseman, he was a member of perhaps the greatest international team ever assembled when he and his Soviet teammates were upset by Team USA in the "Miracle Game" in Lake Placid, Slava Fetisov was on the NHL's radar.

In fact, he was drafted in 1978 (12th round, 201st overall) by the Montreal Canadiens, then the most dominant NHL franchise by a country mile. Oh, and they were coached by Scotty Bowman. Coincidence that he was at the draft table when the Habs made that pick? There are no coincidences in hockey, eh?

At any rate, with the Iron Curtain still standing and the Soviet Union still mighty, there was no way Fetisov was getting a pass to play in the NHL. So he was re-entered into the draft, and in 1983 the Devils took a flyer, selecting Fetisov in the eighth round (145th overall and eight picks after Montreal had taken all-world goaltender Vladislav Tretiak).

It took six stressful years during which Fetisov challenged the Soviet system, was exiled to a do-nothing Army job, and went public on national TV expressing his outrage and displeasure with the iron-fisted, ham-handed Soviet officials governing sports in his country, before he finally won his release to play hockey in North America.

By then he was 31 years old, his best years behind him. And when he finally walked into the Devils' locker room, he was immediately outcast by most of his teammates who were threatened by Soviet players arriving to take their jobs. Nevertheless, he scored 8 goals among 42 points in 1989-90 and had five strong seasons in New Jersey despite having to play a game that was completely foreign to him.

Coaches ragged him for holding the puck in order to make a play. They implored him to dump the puck into the offensive zone—a mortal sin among his Soviet teammates. Things got better when his former Red Army teammate Alexei Kasatonov arrived and, as defense partners, they found their own comfort level.

By the time the Red Wings acquired him for a third-round draft pick in early 1995, Fetisov was approaching 37. But Bowman, who executed that deal with the Devils, finally got his man, even though his players in Detroit didn't know what to make of it, including The Captain.

Here's Steve Yzerman:

It was intriguing for us because he was a pretty big name. I didn't know him, but I certainly knew of him. I'd played against him, but I didn't know whether he was playing or not playing [in New Jersey], so I was very curious. And when he came in and he got on the ice with us, very quickly we were like, "Hey, this guy's pretty good, you know?"

He could move the puck, he's really smart, and he's big, a big thick guy. And you know, his personality was awesome right off the bat. He was the guy right in the middle of all the conversations, the dinners, the card games, a very outgoing guy. Very funny, very personable, and just a real gentleman as well, to everyone. He was a hit as soon as he joined the locker room.

And Slava is a leader, for sure. No nonsense. Him, and Igor as well, these were the older guys; they were strong leaders. They were very smart guys, and they weren't afraid to speak their minds—whether it was Kozzie, Vladdie, or even Sergei, for that matter. They were like, "Guys, this is the way it is. This is what we're doing." And they set a great example for them.

Even later on, Pavel Datsyuk comes in and Igor's still there at the time, and he set an example for Pavel. Those younger guys all looked up to them. They were legends when they were growing up, and now they got a chance to play with them. They were a real, extremely positive influence.

So, yeah, for us players when trades were made we didn't spend a lot of time, at least back then, analyzing them. I didn't even know exactly what Slava was traded for. For us players, a second- or third-round pick meant nothing. It was just, "We're getting a defenseman," and initially we're not sure what that meant to our team.

But Slava and Igor, they still had the skill and they still had the knowledge. Now they were getting a chance to play with the young, fresh legs, and I think that invigorated them. That combination of tremendously skilled, fast young guys with the experience and knowledge of the veterans—that was a great combination. You put the five of them together and it worked out pretty well.

A 'Mr. Hockey' Welcome to Detroit

In December 1978, a team of Soviet All-Stars made a six-game tour of World Hockey Association teams. A young, powerful Slava Fetisov, then a teenager for a few more months, was among them. And when the Soviets played the New England Whalers, Fetisov had the audacity to lay one of his patented hip checks on a guy named Gordie Howe.

With thighs the size of tree trunks, a sizable derriere of pure muscle, and the ability to skate backward better than some players could skate forward, Fetisov could put a quick end to someone's career with that play. And many years later, Howe reminded him of that.

"Gordie Howe, he was there for my first game in Detroit," Fetisov recalled. "He shake my hand and he said, 'Slava, welcome!' Then he remind me when I hip-check him. There was a big fight after this because he was too old to be body-checked from the young kid. But you know, that was memories in a good way."

For the record, Howe was 50 years old then. He had 34 goals among 96 points in 76 games that season for the Whalers.

*Fetisov's best years were behind him by the time he got to Detroit;
he would turn 37 a few months after he was traded to the Wings
by New Jersey. Turns out, he still had some good hockey left in him.*

―――――――●―――――――

Dave Lewis coached the Wings' defensemen:

All I know is, when Slava Fetisov came from New Jersey to the Detroit Red Wings, he was so much better than I thought he was. I watched him on film when we had played against him, so I can only imagine 10 years prior to that how great he was at the highest level every night. And that was when every night somebody wanted to skewer your eyes out, cross-check you in one of these international tournaments—when the Red Machine was hated globally by all hockey teams.

I think the players were a bit surprised. We had talked about it, and we were thinking, *Why are we getting a veteran guy who hasn't played much in New Jersey when we want to get faster or more rugged or whatever?* Because that was always the problem. We were either too skilled or not tough enough. So we're adding another skilled player. But it turned out he wasn't just a skilled player; he was a rugged physical warrior who was relentless. And it was a bit of a surprise to everybody once he started to get in shape and once he started to get everybody together to play that style.

Scotty knew what he would bring to the Russian players we had at the time, and he was exactly right. Once Slava walked into the room, besides getting the respect of the players who had played against him in the international tournaments, the Yzermans, the Lidstroms, the Shanahans, guys like that—as soon as Slava came in, the Russian guys, they didn't bow, but they really respected him for who he was and the things that he could help them with. And that was probably one of the biggest reasons Scotty brought him, knowing that this was going to have an effect on the players, the young Russian players that we had.

For instance, Sergei [Fedorov] at times can be a hard person to talk to, to influence. But I know that Slava Fetisov had no problem influencing Sergei. There was a mutual respect, but Slava was still the boss. His word was written in stone almost.

On That Notorious Hip Check

One thing many of us came to appreciate about Brendan Shana-
han is that he is a lifelong learner. He paid attention to everything,
stored it all away, broke it all down, analyzed it and compartmen-
talized it for the future, whenever he might need it.

As a young player in the NHL, he had a front-row seat during the
Russian invasion into the NHL, and when you listen to him talk
it's clear that some of what he saw sickened his stomach. But it
didn't take him long to admire and respect the fight Slava Fetisov
put up to survive, and thrive, in the NHL.

Here's Brendan Shanahan:

I don't remember if it was Slava's first game or just early in his tenure in New Jersey, but he got into it with Wendel Clark in Toronto. I
don't know that they fought as much as there was a scrum and Wendel
dropped the gloves and gave Slava a black eye.

Now if you know Slava, he's a very proud guy. And he's a great
checker, a great *hip* checker. He could've done that in every game if he
wanted to. As a matter of fact, he did it a couple of times in training

camp to our own players and we had to go to him, you know, not in the most gentle of ways, and explain to him like, "That doesn't fly in here." If you're going to hip check a guy, especially your own guy, in practice, you're going to have four other guys jumping on your back.

But he was so good at it. He could skate backward so fast, and get so low, and he was a big man. I think he just decided, "Okay, it's an unwritten code," and he would look at us like we're crazy. The hip check is part of the game, but if there's an unwritten code, you can't hip heck, you don't hip check, so he had stopped doing that.

So anyway, Wendel had embarrassed him. Slava didn't speak a lot of English, but I think he circled the date that Toronto came to New Jersey next. I happened to be on the ice, in the Toronto zone, and we turned the puck over. Their defensemen made a pass to Wendel coming out of the zone, and I was behind Wendel or beside him, somewhere near him. And it was almost like, I didn't see it, but I could feel the speed and how low and fast Slava Fetisov was coming at Wendel. Ass first, about three feet off the ice. So low, and he was going to take out both of Wendel's knees.

It was fast and it was powerful, and Wendel saw him at the last second and got 90 percent out of the way. They ended up, you know, squaring off. Wendel sort of limped over to him, and Slava wanted to fight him, and I remember thinking, *Okay, I'm going to jump in here and fight.* But there was something about Slava's face that he wanted to fight Wendel, that he wanted to be a man.

So we stopped; we backed off. Sure enough, Wendel grabbed him, hit him once. Slava wasn't used to fighting, so he fell to the ice and then we all jumped in. But Slava got up from that fight and he was just fine. Wendel limped off and probably missed 4 to 6 months with a torn ligament. If he didn't get 90 percent out of the way, Slava might have ended his career right then and there. So, yes, Slava was a pretty proud guy.

A lot of the older [North American] players were angry when the Russians were coming over. You know, the feeling was they're taking jobs. Nobody said that about Swedes, but I'm sure there was a day when they did. Borje Salming went through that in Toronto. But it was just different when the Swedes were coming over, and the Finns.

With the Russians, it was a lot of talk of, you know, Commies; they were the enemy. And now they're over here and taking jobs from good ol' Canadian and American kids. It was a little bit more of an old-school view.

I remember that he wasn't treated well by everybody, including NHL officials, some, not all of them, and some coaches and players. Unlike some of the players who defected to get over here, Fetisov wanted to walk out the front door. He wanted his freedom. He didn't want to defect even when they gave him opportunities to defect. He wouldn't do it, so they tried to embarrass him in many ways. It's why I have so much respect for Fetisov.

But he looked tired. He *was* tired when he first came over in New Jersey, and I thought that maybe they had worn him down too much before he came over.

When I saw him in Detroit years later, there were two things that were very different: One is, we just played a style that was more conducive to the game he knew, and it helped that he had the other Russians to play with. But he didn't just have success with the Russian Five; he had success with the way Scotty Bowman coached the team, which was puck possession.

I remember having a beer with him, maybe sitting on the plane or going to dinner one night, and I just said to him, like, "Papa Bear, why are you so good again? How did this happen? We used to see you come in some mornings in New Jersey and we just . . . It looked like you needed some sleep." He explained to me, and at that point his English was good enough, everything that had been done to him in Russia, that we're all just learning now, and the struggle he went through.

And he got here and said, "Okay, I'm free. I've got my freedom. I'm coming to the NHL." He didn't anticipate the struggle he was about to face from people taking cheap shots at him, and teammates not necessarily having his back, and officials sometimes turning a blind eye to certain things that were happening to him. It took him a few years to adjust.

I was lucky enough to be in my second year in New Jersey when Fetisov came over. I was just so honored to meet him and play with him. I just thought then, and then thought again when I was reunited with him in Detroit, and still think when I see him now, that he's just a king of a man, on and off the ice.

The Epitome of Professionalism

Nicklas Lidstrom is arguably the greatest defenseman in the history of the game. Even Bobby Orr, widely considered the greatest ever for the way he changed the position and singlehandedly transformed the game, concedes it's a worthy debate.

While we can argue that ad nauseum, there is no disputing the fact that Lidstrom, whether or not he needed them, had some marvelous mentors in his early years in Detroit. Brad McCrimmon was an early defense partner. And there were Hall-of-Famers like Mark Howe, Paul Coffey, and Larry Murphy. An Olympic gold medalist, Mike Ramsey, an anchor on that "Miracle" team, was also there in the back of the room among the defensemen when Lidstrom was a youngster.

Then along came a guy with Hall of Fame credentials and two Olympic gold medals (and a silver he hates talking about). But Slava Fetisov was on Lidstrom's radar long before either of them got to Detroit.

Here's the Perfect Human, Nick Lidstrom:

When we first traded for Slava, I was just thrilled to be able to play with him because as a little kid I watched him and the Soviet Union dominate in the hockey world. So I was excited. I knew we added a player with a lot of character. Slava's got, you know, he was the captain of the Soviet National Team. And I think he helped us right off the bat when he came, with his presence in the room and on the ice as well.

What I learned from Slava was his professionalism, showing up at work every day and being really serious about his job, the way he carried himself: "This is my job. This is what I do for a living." You know, we all did that, but he really showed it. He showed that he didn't take anything for granted. He was working hard every night. There he is, getting older, he's getting up there in age, but he's still being a professional about it, being a pro. And just being around it, you see a player of his caliber, at his age, and he's still bringing it every night, every day at practice too, and that helped me just being around that environment.

Slava Fetisov was probably the best defenseman outside of the NHL when I watched him throughout the '80s, the way he would dominate games. Whether it would be bringing the puck up the ice and doing it on his own, or making a pass and making his teammates look good, he was the total package. He had a strong presence on the ice. You couldn't fight him off the puck.

But he had to adjust to a different kind of game where you're dumping the puck in a lot more, with a lot more physical players, in smaller rinks. We're playing a little bit different game in the NHL, so I think it was hard on him. And players took runs at him because he was from the Soviet Union. He was one of the first at breaking the barrier to come over here, and I'm sure it was very tough on him.

When he first came to the NHL and the Devils, he was a target. From what I heard, some of his teammates would kind of freeze him out too. So he was really facing an uphill battle throughout his first couple of seasons over here. When he came to Detroit, he had a couple of seasons under his belt, but what he went through I think showed why he was working so hard. I think that's why he didn't take anything for granted, because he had a tough time in his first couple years in the NHL.

The Genius of Scotty Bowman

Adjusting to a new culture, learning a new language in North America—those paled in comparison to having to master a fundamentally different style of play in the National Hockey League. And Slava Fetisov is the first to admit that he didn't understand why NHL coaches insisted he just shoot the puck into the offensive zone so his teammates could rush in and fight for possession of it again.

"If I was gonna dump it in for [Sergei] Makarov or [Igor] Larionov, once, all right," Fetisov told John U. Bacon of The Detroit News. "Two times, they get pissed off. Third time, they say, 'You go in and get it.' But in NHL, I get so much heat for holding the puck. The forwards would skate away from me, and I still have puck. I look like idiot!"

There's a better way, the Russians insisted, and occasionally they insisted so much that they'd reach an impasse with their coaches, and it would be time to move on. That's eventually what happened in San Jose, where Igor Larionov could no longer work under Coach Kevin Constantine and asked to be traded. That's when General Manager Dean Lombardi picked up the phone and made a call to Detroit.

Here's Dave Lewis:

Igor has told me this story: He played for a coach who wanted him to dump the puck in and Igor wouldn't do it, even in practice. The coach would blow the whistle, call him over, and tell him, "I told you to dump the puck in." Igor's response was, "I'm not a big guy. I work so hard to get the puck. I'm not going to get rid of it and then go try to get it again."

For him it makes sense. So, in their mindset, all five [Russian] guys began to think as one when they were together. When they were separated, they would play our system. And maybe that's what Scotty was referring to. He wouldn't let the other players play like that because, first of all, they're not trained to play like that. And second, they don't know where to go at the right time like the Russian Five do.

But you could take the Russian Five and take one of them and put them with another four guys and they would play the American game to a point where you couldn't tell the difference.

That was the genius of Scotty Bowman. He was never afraid to try something. And if he tried something, he had the credibility that if some naysayer would look at it and shake their head and say this would never work, well, they never said that to Scotty because of his stature in the game.

He has vision. I don't know where it comes from, but he has vision that none of us have. And I think this was one of the moments in the history of the game where Scotty, by bringing those guys together, they just got better and better, and we ended up winning the Stanley Cup.

Creating Masterpieces

I first met and interviewed Igor Larionov on October 7, 1989, after the morning skate prior to his second NHL game with the Vancouver Canucks. I had stopped him on his way to the locker room at the Pacific Coliseum, where he and his teammates would be playing the Red Wings later that night. (He would later have two assists in a 5-2 Vancouver victory.)

Larionov couldn't have been more gracious with his time or his willingness to try to answer any and all my questions. He was a bit guarded, but then again that was a natural trait of any player produced under the Soviet system; they are careful in the extreme about what they say because they trust no one. But I couldn't shake the feeling, listening between the lines of his words, that he wasn't entirely happy. Maybe it was the culture shock. More likely it was the system of hockey he was forced to play, or the kinds of ugly incidents he had endured even in the preseason against opponents who hated him merely for his Russian DNA.

We crossed paths several times during the first round of the Stanley Cup playoffs in 1994, when Larionov led the San Jose Sharks to that monumental seven-game upset of the Red Wings, nearly everyone's pick to advance to the Finals that year. But it wasn't until that fall, in Moscow, that I had the opportunity for another, more in-depth one-on-one conversation.

That was during the NHL's first labor stoppage. The players had been locked out by the owners, the season in jeopardy. But Larionov partnered with his old Red Army teammate Slava Fetisov in New Jersey, and together they hatched a plan to take a team of former Soviet stars—by now there were dozens of them in the NHL—back to Russia for a handful of games in a three-week barnstorming tour.

Larionov arranged the financing, aided by a sponsorship from Sun Microsystems, a Silicon Valley company. Fetisov greased the skids politically, which was a little tricky because that team of Russians included two young defectors, Buffalo's Alexander Mogilny and Detroit's Sergei Fedorov. That's two-thirds of a forward line that, with Pavel Bure, was groomed to lead the powerful Red Army Club for another decade of dominance.

It was there that I first encountered Fetisov for the privilege of a private conversation. He too was gracious but guarded in his responses as he struggled with a language he was still trying to master. But in Moscow I saw a completely different Larionov— outgoing, talkative, jovial. I couldn't help but think that being back home with so many of his friends and former teammates—all of them experiencing freedoms that they could never have imagined in the system they left behind—was the difference from when I'd first met him in Vancouver.

He even made a point to send a locker room attendant out and bring me in after a game to do my work as I was used to in North America. He patted a space next to him on the bench, inviting me to sit and talk. Our relationship at that moment began to turn into something warm, respectful, and most important, trusting—and still always professional.

Needless to say, I was beyond thrilled when I learned that Scotty Bowman had pulled the trigger on a deal that would bring a fifth former Red Army Club player to Detroit.

Igor Larionov remembers it well:

Well, I was in San Jose. I was sitting in my house for two weeks because I asked for a trade. I was training with Silicon Valley executives, trying to keep myself in shape. It was seven in the morning in San Jose, 10 o'clock in Detroit, when I got a phone call. I pick up the phone and I hear, "This is Scotty Bowman and we just made a trade. They traded you to Detroit."

Then he asked some questions, like what number would I want to wear, how many kids in the family, stuff like that. And then he said he would like me to join the team in the next couple of days. I was obviously surprised. And I was happy too, because they traded me for Ray Shephard.

Then I hear that one of the guys from the newsroom, he was a media guy working for the *Detroit Free Press* or the *Detroit News*, he said, "Who is Larionov? A 35-year-old guy, and we trade a 50-goal scorer?"

But instead of going to Detroit, Scotty said to meet the team in western Canada. The first game was in Canada. He said to be there the day before the game, meet the boys, the team.

So I came to Calgary and [assistant coaches] Dave Lewis and Barry Smith, they met me in the hotel lobby and said, "Igor, would you maybe come up to the room to talk about the system, what type of hockey we play?" And I said, "Yeah, of course." I am only happy to see what is going on, so we went to the room to talk and they told about the left-wing lock, which was Detroit's defensive system. I told them that everything is understandable.

And they say, "Well, you know, you five guys, you figure out yourself how to play." So in the first game in Calgary, they announced the five Russian guys would be playing the first time together in the National Hockey League for the Detroit Red Wings. And we came out and we played an outstanding game, the whole team did.

We did not have much time to practice, only like morning skate before the game. I was the last who joined that unit, the line, but we clicked right away when we played as a group, had a great time on the ice. And you know the rest of the story. We start to win more games, we start to make some noise in Hockeytown, and the fans start to understand, like, this is a brand-new style of hockey. It was like a chain reaction because everybody else on the team started to follow this kind of style. And we started to play more like the team that is not going to give away the puck easily.

Obviously those guys had already been playing really good, the Red Wings, and you could see this new generation of players doing some good things, individually and as a team. They were a top team in the league, but at the same time there was, like, an extra mile we needed to go to be successful, to put everything together to get to the next level, like a serious commitment and a goal that will get us through tough days and good days.

We needed to be consistent, and that is what I think Slava brought from New Jersey and what I brought from San Jose. Our goal was to bring that to the Russian Five, that whole Soviet experience and knowledge to everybody, to lead by example. We can make a difference in the game. That is what Slava and I were trying to do. I was trying to take care of the forwards. Slava was on defense with Vladdie.

We were trying to glue everybody together and then perform as a unit, as a kind of mini-team. Like five of us to go and create some offense, create some masterpieces—and win hockey games.

The Diesel That Led

If you twirled a hockey stick in the center of the Red Wings'
locker room and let it fall, it was bound to be pointing at a leader.
It seemed there was a born leader of men in almost every stall—
from Steve Yzerman to Brendan Shanahan, Nick Lidstrom and
Kris Draper.

There were also a couple of former captains of the Soviet National
team and Red Army Club: Slava Fetisov and his successor, Vlad-
imir Konstantinov. But in that room at that time, Konstanti-
nov deferred respectfully to Fetisov as the two Russian forwards
of his generation, Sergei Fedorov and Slava Kozlov, deferred to
Igor Larionov.

And what unfolded around that locker room, especially in the wake
of the tragic limo accident, was something special to witness.

Dave Lewis says so:

S lava Fetisov, being the warrior that he was, and Igor Larionov, being
the player that he was—both Hall-of-Famers—they performed

better than what anybody thought they could perform that season, and especially in the playoffs. They were the diesel that led. They were the train that pulled everybody else with them, and everybody followed.

Stevie was the captain, but Fetisov and Larionov had a closer connection to Vladdie, where he came from and what he went through. They were the driving force.

I remember coaching the Russian Five through the years, how they would come back to the bench as a group of five, maybe during a time-out, or an official or someone would be fixing the ice. They'd come back and lean against the boards, and every now and then Slava Fetisov would start to yell at them.

He wasn't really yelling at Igor. He was maybe yelling at Sergei, then Sergei would turn around and yell at Slava Kozlov, and then Slava Kozlov would yell at Vladimir Konstantinov, then Vladdie would yell something back. But it always seemed to trickle down from either Igor or Slava Fetisov down to the other guys.

And it seemed to me that Vladdie was always the one who was getting dumped on. They would say everything in Russian so we didn't know what they were talking about. It was always about performance, some particular play, a missed assignment on the ice. But it seemed comical. But nobody ever yelled at Fetisov. And they rarely yelled at Larionov. The other three seemed to get most of the abuse, the younger guys.

Legends in the Stalls Nearby

Kris Draper, the centerpiece of the iconic Grind Line, was far more than an energy guy who could kick in the odd huge goal when it mattered most. While he morphed into a key front-office executive with the Wings when his playing days concluded, he was always an avid fan and serious historian of the game as it was played around the world.

He paid attention. He learned. And when some of the most celebrated Soviet stars began showing up in stalls just a few seats away from his in the Detroit Red Wings' dressing room, he was mesmerized.

Here's Kris Draper:

You know what? I was actually a pretty lucky kid. As a 16-year-old, I watched the Canada Cup in Hamilton. I was able to see the KLM line [Igor Larionov centering Vladimir Krutov and Sergei Makarov] with [Slava] Fetisov and [Alexei] Kasatonov on the back end. As a 17-year-old kid, I played against the Russian Red Army team, and I never touched the puck.

Now all of a sudden you throw those guys [the Russian Five] out there and it was the same thing. It was magical what they were doing, how they were playing, you know, throwing pucks into space, the regrouping. And to me, probably the greatest thing is that they were having so much fun. That was the amazing thing.

You put these guys who all grew up in the same system, now you're putting them in the National Hockey League, and they were able to bring how they played as kids and how they played, obviously, as early adults and they were able to do that in the NHL. No one had ever done that before. You saw spurts of it with two or three players at a time, but all of a sudden you put five guys out there and these guys were magical with what they did with the puck.

Sometimes you're just on the bench and you just kind of, you know, you couldn't help yourself; you kind of laughed a little bit at what they were doing. But you know, the one thing Scotty made sure of is that no other line was allowed to do that, especially my line. We had to make sure we're getting pucks deep. Don't even think about regrouping.

I think that's what made our team special going into the mid to late '90s. We had so many different looks. You know, we had the Russian Five the way they could control the puck; we had Steve Yzerman, who at the time was evolving as the greatest leader in our sport, a great two-way hockey player; we had the Grind Line, and you know they all played different.

There were a lot of things that complemented the Detroit Red Wings, but the Russian Five were—it was a treat to watch on most nights. It was unbelievable what these guys did.

You know, a lot of guys in that room grew up kind of idolizing Igor and Slava and everything they stood for. I know I couldn't get enough of the stories that they could tell. I don't even know if we got them all, but it was amazing, everything they went through in the [Anatoly] Tarasov days, the early training they had back in Russia, and obviously the Viktor Tikhonov days and the success they had.

Then, you know, the Miracle on Ice game in 1980, Slava was a part of that defeat, which we know is one of the biggest upsets in the history of sports. I think that shaped him as a person and as a leader. And now you have him coming into the dressing room and you have young players like a Fedorov, Kozlov and a Konstantinov, so they could always have somebody to ask questions to, someone to lean on.

That's important, no matter what, when you have teammates that you know you can trust. And I think these guys challenged themselves. I really believe they wanted to win together, and that's something special. You could see the excitement, especially after we won in 1997.

I've talked to Slava numerous times about when went up to Mr. Bettman and said, "You know we want to bring the Stanley Cup to Moscow now." I don't think the reaction was a favorable one at first, but obviously we all know that it went over there and what an experience that was. You know these guys made a lasting impression on Sergei, on Kozzie, on Vladdie, just because of everything that they did.

They basically opened up the doors for all those guys to come to the National Hockey League and live out their dreams at a young age. Obviously Slava and Igor lived out their dream, but it took a lot for that to happen—a lot of pressure and a lot of things to go right for that to happen.

And when they got here, they made everybody better. That's what elite hockey players do. You're surrounded by great people and great hockey players and you see the way they play, you see the way they compete night in and night out, and then in the morning they're in the gym preparing to play another game.

That was a special environment that the Detroit Red Wings had going into the late '90s into the early 2000s.

The Difference in an
Epic Playoff Sweep

Since Brendan Shanahan is about to elaborate, let's recap a few details about that remarkable second-round Stanley Cup playoff series against Anaheim in the spring of 1997: This was the first-ever post-season meeting between the two clubs, and it ended in a four-game sweep—after 18 periods of hockey.

In the opening game, Sergei Fedorov's third-period goal sent the game into OT, which lasted 59 seconds before Martin Lapointe ended it.

Game 2 ended at 1:30 of the third overtime period on a goal by Slava Kozlov, with assists from Vladimir Konstantinov and Slava Fetisov.

Game 3 was a veritable rout, 5-3. The Russians accounted for four of the goals, two by Kozlov and one each by Igor Larionov and Sergei Fedorov. The Russians also has six of the eight assists awarded, three by Konstantinov and two by Fedorov. The Wings had a stranglehold on the series, but the Mighty Ducks weren't going to go easily.

Game 4 ended at 17:03 of the second overtime on a goal by Sha-nahan. Fedorov was the lone Russian to show up on the score-board, with an assist on a momentum-changing tying goal by Doug Brown late in the first period.

To all involved, the series felt more like a seven-game grind than a four-game sweep. And Shanahan wasn't shy about highlighting the importance of the Russians in that series—especially the guy most people tend to overlook.

●————————————●

Here's Brendan Shanahan:

In that first year's ['97] playoffs, the series that I remember the Rus-sians really coming together for us was the Anaheim series, where they played a lot of the time together in a couple of those games and won some games for us. They just had some really big nights.

Scotty didn't put them together all the time, and I think that was the genius of Scotty, because the other teams had to prepare for it. He had a lot of other line combinations he would use. And I can think back to every one of those games from that one playoff year and we wouldn't have won the Stanley Cup if it wasn't for one of those five at a certain moment.

If you look at a lot of our big goals, tying goals, overtime goals, game-winning goals in each series, you see one or two of those guys directly involved. And one, Kozlov, was one of the most underrated snipers around. He was also a mean, ornery guy.

He was ornery with us. He didn't like it if you said good-morning to him. He'd just look at you as if it were a silly salutation, you know? Grumpy Kozlov. We all had fun with him.

And he was a dirty player, but an extremely skilled player. That guy, if I had to list a guy on my team that I wanted to have the puck in the slot, that I had confidence that the puck was going in, it's Slava Kozlov.

A Generational Shift

From the moment the Red Wings dove headfirst into the European-player pool until they paraded the Stanley Cup down Woodward Avenue with 1.2 million witnesses to the celebration, there were hard-core skeptics. Some were in the Detroit locker room, others in the media, and legions of fans—especially in Canada, where people guard the game and its traditions as a kind of birthright.

It began in 1989 with a draft that not only transformed the Wings' roster almost immediately but also pushed the rest of the NHL to keep up or get left behind—which happened to some teams that dismissed the importance of diversifying their rosters. The league, after all, had designs on growing dramatically, by more than a third, from 21 teams to 30 in nine years, from 1991 to 2000. The smartest teams figured out pretty quickly that if they wanted to compete they needed to expand their horizons beyond North America, where the talent pool started getting quite shallow after the first couple of rounds of the draft. So they followed Detroit's lead, growing their European scouting staffs while setting aside some of their hard-core biases against imports from across the pond.

As an assistant coach in Detroit, Dave Lewis had a front-row seat to the revolution that changed the National Hockey League—for the better.

Here's Dave Lewis:

Okay, so you go to the draft to get the best players possible to help the team, and in Detroit we were drafting Russians, Swedes, and some other European players. And the mentality in our locker room was similar to the mentality around the National Hockey League—but not everybody, as there were some players who were unhappy with "all these Russians, these Europeans."

They knew these guys were going to come in and compete for positions, for their jobs. They thought we should be focusing more on North Americans [in the draft]. That mentality persisted that you can't win with a Russian player and you could never win with two Russian players. And Swedes were really soft. Czech players were supposed to be really selfish.

But all those barriers were broken down with this group of Russian players. I truly believe that the acceptance of Steve Yzerman of these guys was probably the biggest door that was opened. Now the rest of the players had to face up to them also. But they [Russians and Swedes] also had to perform at a high level. There was no cheating, no favors, no shortcuts, because everybody in that locker room was there for one reason, and that was to win the Stanley Cup.

As good as they were, though, the Russians were not well liked around the National Hockey League because they were taking jobs away from our boys, Canadian and U.S. players. So if you saw a Russian you were going to slash him, try to intimidate him, cross check him, show him no respect whatsoever. I've heard of players spitting on Russians, breaking their ankles, just a lot of nasty things that you wouldn't normally do to a young player coming from Saskatchewan.

In Detroit, though, our mentality was basically, why wouldn't we look all over the world to get the best players available to us to compete at the highest level for the Stanley Cup?

And then, wow! You know, the thing I do remember so vividly is the Stanley Cup parade in '97. Everybody was together; we were in these cars. It was a generational thing, looking at the fans. You saw a grandfather with his son and daughter, maybe and grandkids and aunts and uncles. It wasn't just a couple watching; it was generations.

I think those guys, the Russian Five and the rest of the players, brought that out, not just in Detroit but throughout Michigan. They brought that unity, that hope. The team had struggled for so many years, and sometimes life is a struggle, you know? But we found a way to achieve that success, with people telling us it was impossible to win with Russians.

I remember talking to a reporter right after we had won the Stanley Cup at Joe Louis Arena. I was sort of saying to all those naysayers, right there in front of the camera, asking, "Well, what are you going to say now?"

It was a special moment.

'I Can't Believe I Shook His . . .'

By almost any calibration, the 1995-96 season was a resounding success. Rebounding from a shocking four-game sweep in the Stanley Cup Finals at the hands of the New Jersey Devils the previous spring, the Red Wings were hell-bent on making sure that wouldn't happen again.

They took no prisoners in a record-smashing 62-win season, two more than the 1976-77 Montreal Canadiens. Their 131 points were one shy of the 132 that the Habs team earned, but 27 more than Colorado in a runaway race to win their second straight President's Trophy.

But hardly anyone remembers any of that. All people tend to talk about is the brutal, sickening, and disgusting way that season ultimately ended well short of the goal—again. And no one more so than this guy.

Here's Kris Draper:

Obviously, I took a pretty nasty hit there. We were at McNichol's Arena, and at the time there were two dressing rooms, one where you changed out of your regular clothes and into your workout stuff and the other was where you got dressed to go out on the ice.

After the game, I was in the other room; that's where the doctors were set up. The guys didn't really know the extent of my injuries, and after the game I think everything was magnified because of the fact that we did lose and they're going on to the Stanley Cup Finals and we're not.

And then my teammates saw how I was, the condition I was in, and it fired up a lot of guys. When you see teammates like that, you tend to rally around that moment, and the guys did that. And it kind of goes to what I said about how we were evolving as a team and the friendships and how the on-ice stuff was carrying to the off-ice stuff.

We really truly had a lot of great friends on that team, but we weren't able to win. After that, well, you can go back to some of the interviews afterward with some of the players, most notably Dino Ciccarelli. He was furious about how things went on, and he had some comments about it. We kind of got into a little bit of a war of words, and it went from there.

To me, that hit and that night and all the way through 2002, I would say was the most intense rivalry in professional sports—and it led to some great hockey. You can talk about the fights and whatever you want, but the bottom line is, you look at those two teams and they put a lot of players in the Hockey Hall of Fame. Just great, great teams on both sides.

And to be honest, I would say we were lucky; the nucleus of that team was lucky that it stayed together. But then you think of some of the great players on that team who weren't part of the 1996-97 season when we won the Cup.

But for us, you know, we just felt that [1995-96] it was our year, especially after the upset to San Jose in '94, then getting swept by New Jersey in '95. We felt that we kind of paid the price. We dealt with a lot of tough losses, and we felt, going through the regular season like we did, that we were finding different ways to win hockey games.

Then all of a sudden it's over in six games before we even get to the Finals. We ran into a heck of a hockey team led by Joe Sakic, Petr Forsberg, Patrick Roy, those players. That was a great hockey team. We had some great battles, and unfortunately we just came up short again. It was really, really disappointing that it ended like that, with everything that we accomplished. The most successful season in NHL history, all those wins. We felt we were kind of evolving as a team, evolving as a group—and yet . . .

When you do that, you open the door to a lot of doubters and naysayers. A lot of people questioned the Detroit Red Wings—again. We were too soft. We had too many Europeans. You can't win with Russians. You can't win with Swedes. Our Canadians weren't the right Canadians. There was a lot of stuff being said.

People just doubted the team from top to bottom, and obviously when you don't win, things happen and changes are made. But fortunately, for the nucleus of the team, Scotty [Bowman] believed in us. There were some things that happened, obviously the big trade for Brendan Shanahan. And you know, we went from there.

Then Colorado comes in for that game in March, and it was kind of amazing, everything that happened. We had so many guys thrown out that at one point I was playing defense. I was Nick Lidstrom's partner.

But when we came into the locker room after that game, we kind of knew that we did something special that night—for us. How everything just played out, you know, with the fights, the revenge, Mac scoring the game-winner, us winning the game, all those things—it was a really big moment for the 1997 team.

Friendship in Name Only?

Fairly early in the venomous rivalry between Detroit and Colorado, some players on both sides formed an uneasy truce as teammates when the NHL first authorized its players to compete in the Olympic Games: Steve Yzerman and Brendan Shanahan from the Wings; Joe Sakic, Adam Foote, and Patrick Roy from the Avs.

They actually broke bread together off the ice too. And, yes, they shared some stories about that epic brawl at The Joe on March 26, 1997.

"Patrick Roy told me at dinner once that he had hurt his shoulder when he and I leaped in the air, and that it was sort of permanently damaged a little bit," Shanahan said. "I said I was sorry.

And then Steve Yzerman leaned into my ear and said, 'You're not sorry.' And I said, 'I know I'm not, but we're at dinner and I gotta be polite.' But I did get some joy out of that because Roy was so good, and I did have a lot of respect for him."

Shanahan has always maintained that that game—with Claude Lemieux being pummeled as he turtled beneath the blows from Darren McCarty, then scoring three straight goals to come from behind and win in overtime—gave the Wings a psychological edge that carried them to the Stanley Cup championship a few months later.

But there is far, far more in the backstory to this rivalry. And for Brendan Shanahan, it went way, way back.

———————•———————————•———————

Brendan Shanahan explains:

What was interesting for me, personally, was that I had played with Claude Lemieux in New Jersey—and even that previous summer we were teammates for Team Canada on the World Cup.

He had just had a son, and he made an effort to introduce me to his wife. He explained that when they had their son they were struggling to find a name, and he said to his wife, "You know, I played with this guy in New Jersey and I really like the name 'Brendan.' What do you think of that name?"

So they end up having a son, Brendan. She came over and gave me a hug. I sort of felt like, you know, I felt like they had named the baby after me. Well, maybe not after me. But you know, we were friends.

Well, I go to Detroit and I know that's got to stop, which is fine. I have no problem separating on the ice and off the ice. So I was trying to run Claude Lemieux like everyone else. He's the enemy now. And then, as it worked out . . . it wasn't planned. We didn't say this shift or that shift; it just happened. The right people were on the ice for us at the time, and Igor [Larionov] was centering Darren McCarty and me. And like I said, it just happened that Claude was on the ice.

I don't think Igor started the fight with [Petr] Forsberg because we were on the ice and Lemieux was on the ice. It happened organically. But once it started, I remember Adam Foote gabbed onto McCarty and Mac was . . . I mean it all happened in a second, but Mac was screaming my name and he came over and I knew what he wanted. He wanted to get loose, and Foote had a hold of him.

I sort of knocked Foote's arms free, and Darren went right at Lemieux. And I was happy that I didn't have to go after Lemieux, you know? Because there was a part of me that, as much as I was a Red Wing, I still didn't want to be the guy on top of Claude Lemieux. But Darren took care of that.

And a second later I saw Patrick Roy at the hash marks in full stride. It's an unbelievable scene, what happened next, with all of us jumping in the air. It was like *The Matrix*. We're all fighting. But what's really funny about that brawl, if brawls are funny—and, kids, brawls aren't funny—but back then they were hilarious.

What was really interesting about that brawl was, when the game was over and we had won, we won in overtime and Darren had scored that winning goal, we all piled into the coaches' room to sort of watch the winning goal. But what we really wanted to see were the fights.

Obviously the whole arena saw Mike Vernon and Patrick Roy, and Roy and me coming together in midair. Our whole bench saw it. Colorado's bench saw it. The commentators are going crazy. The whole hockey world was watching. But when Darren saw the replay he was shocked. He had no idea any of it had occurred. He just thought it was him and Lemieux.

He had no idea Vernon was fighting. He had no idea any of this was happening, and he played that whole game thinking that the whole riot was just him on top of Lemieux. He didn't realize there was this big crime scene going on around him while this was happening—with the highlight being little Mike Vernon throwing a wild haymaker and cutting Roy above the eye.

I think a lot of people still call it the biggest game, or the most popular game in Detroit Red Wings history. It brought us together because we won the game, and I don't know it would've brought us together as much if Colorado had won.

There was a moment in the third when it was 4-3 them, and Kamensky, off a draw in our end, fired a puck home to make it 5-3 with maybe ten or twelve minutes left in the game and Patrick Roy in net. You know, the odds are stacked against us coming back. But we scored two goals to tie it up and we went into overtime.

Igor made a great play at the blue line, which sent Darren and me in on a little bit of a break. Darren was able to, amazingly, be the star of the show, scoring the winning goal.

I don't know if that brings our team together as much if we don't also get the victory. It absolutely gave us confidence that we had a psychological edge over them as well. We didn't just win the fights; we won the game. And they were a tough team. They were a great team. They had a lot of tough guys, not just heavyweights, but tough, tough players.

So it's not that we didn't respect them. We just really didn't like them. You know what? We still don't like them very much. And I love that because Ted Lindsay used to tell me how he played in an era when you really didn't like the guys on the other team you were playing against. And for me, as much respect as I had for some of their players, I still just really didn't like them—especially once we got in the playoffs.

The things they were saying about us, the things that they were saying *to* us—they were Stanley Cup champs, and they were calling us losers. They were saying we were chokers and they were right; we were losers.

It pissed us off when they were saying it, but I remember just biting my lip and thinking, *You know what? You're just giving us more incentive.*

And as a matter of fact, my buddy Claude Lemieux looked at me at one point in the playoffs, during Game 1, and he said, "You're a loser. You haven't won a thing." And I remember there was a part of me that just thought, *Thank you. You've just released me from feeling any form of obligation of friendship to you. You're right. You've reminded me that we have to win. None of this matters unless we win!*

So, yeah, we really didn't like those guys.

'Paybacks Are a Bitch'

Besides owning the whistle in that epic battle between the Red Wings and Colorado Avalanche on March 26, 1997, referee Paul Devorski officiated a number of memorable games at Joe Louis Arena.

The son of Ukrainian and Irish immigrants who settled in Guelph, Ontario, Devorski was one of two refs to preside over Stanley Cup Finals series games between Detroit and Pittsburgh in 2008 (when the Wings won) and 2009 (when the Wings lost).

He also had the honor of officiating some classic international games, including the men's Bronze Medal Game in the 2010 Vancouver Olympic Games, and the men's Gold Medal Game between Sweden and Finland in the 2006 Winter Games in Torino, Italy.

His career highlight? "Man, I have to say that Gold Medal Game in Toronto," he said after a pause. "That was such an honor.

After that, to this day, that Detroit game is No. 2."

That Detroit game, eh? We all remember that one. But Devorski was in the eye of that hurricane, and for the first time he tells his side of that story here.

The morning after one of the most challenging, chaotic—and memorable—games of his career, referee Paul Devorski's phone rang, just as he suspected it would.

He had a good idea who might be calling, and he was right. The big boss, Brian Burke, was on the other end. Not good. Devorski knew what was coming.

"Devo," said Burke, then the NHL's executive vice president and director of hockey operations—and the league's chief disciplinarian, "do you think you might have been able to call *just a few more* penalties last night?"

"Well, yeah," Devorski acknowledged. "I guess I maybe could have, sure."

"Okay," Burke responded. "Just checking."

And that was the end of it, to Devorski's immense relief. But the message was received in no uncertain terms.

The night before, he had called 148 penalty minutes in the fourth and final regular-season matchup between the Detroit Red Wings and the Colorado Avalanche—to the surprise of absolutely no one who was paying even remote attention to hockey in those days.

The Red Wings had a score to settle dating to the previous spring, when the teams met in the Western Conference Finals of the Stanley Cup tournament. In a Game 6 that the Wings needed to win to stay alive, Avs forward Claude Lemieux hit a defenseless Kris Draper from behind. Draper fell forward, hitting his face on the dasher boards right in front of the Detroit bench. The result: a broken jaw, fractured cheekbone, broken nose, damage to his right orbital bone, several missing or broken teeth—and, at least temporarily, the ruination of Draper's ever-present smile.

Eventually, the Avs added insult to injury, scoring the final three goals against a shaken Detroit team to dispatch the Wings. They advanced to the Finals and swept the Florida Panthers for their first Stanley Cup title in franchise history.

"I can't believe I shook his fucking hand," Detroit's Dino Ciccarelli said later, referring to hockey's time-honored series-ending tradition—which pretty much summed up how all of Detroit felt about the cheap-shot artist who rearranged Draper's face.

Lemieux was slapped with a checking-from-behind major and ejection with a game-misconduct penalty. Burke suspended him for two games. Draper took his meals through a straw for the better part of the off-season as his wounds healed around a broken jaw that had been wired shut.

The teams had played each other three times previously without serious incident, but everyone knew that if the Wings were ever going to have their revenge, it would be in this game. Certainly Brian Lewis, the NHL's supervisor of officials, knew it. He's the one who created the schedule for officials. Devorski, with his two experienced linesmen, got their assignment for the game in Detroit about five weeks in advance. But early that afternoon, Lewis phoned Devorski to give him the heads-up that this likely would be a difficult game to officiate.

"Just be ready," Lewis told him. "These teams really don't like each other."

Which explains why Devorski did more tossing and turning than resting as he tried to take his customary pre-game nap.

The NHL didn't institute a two-referee system until the start of the 1999-2000 season, so Devorski would essentially be the sole judge, jury, and executioner in this game. It was a power he took seriously, a power he wielded resolutely—and it would ultimately have far-reaching implications.

Less than five minutes into the game, tensions flared in a battle of defensemen when Detroit's Jamie Pushor fought Colorado's Brent Severyn. At about the halfway mark of the period, forwards Kirk Maltby of Detroit fought the Avs's Rene Corbet.

Then all hell broke loose at 18:22, when Detroit's Igor Larionov, who had had just about enough of Peter Forsberg sticking him from behind as he was trying to carry the puck, finally turned and with a gloved fist threw the first and only punches of his Hall of Fame career. The two fell to the ice, tangled up. Forsberg injured himself and wouldn't return to the game.

But in that serendipitous moment, Darren McCarty looked around the ice, saw Lemieux, and made a beeline, only to be intercepted by Avs defenseman Adam Foote. But as the two squared off, McCarty was calling for reinforcements. No, he didn't need help fighting Foote. Rather, McCarty had a promise to keep, and this was his opportunity.

Immediately, Brendan Shanahan tapped McCarty on the shoulder and said he'd take this dance with Foote. And McCarty turned his savage, pent-up attention toward Lemieux, who immediately submitted, falling to his knees and covering his head with his arms in the classic turtle position.

If Lemieux thought McCarty might hold back since he was essentially surrendering the fight, he was regrettably mistaken. Using his right hand to pull Lemieux up from the ice, McCarty landed several punches to the face and head before dragging Lemieux to the boards directly in front of the Wings bench—giving his best pal Draper a front-row seat—then kneed Lemieux in the head, leaving him lying there in a thickening, sickening pool of blood.

Of the three on-ice officials that night, Devorski was the lowest-ranking member by seniority. He was in his eighth season. Linesman Ray Scapinello, later inducted into the Hockey Hall of Fame, was in his twenty-sixth season, and his partner, Dan Schachte, was in his fifteenth.

The two had their hands full, with all twelve players on the ice paired off. The main the undercard among all those bouts was at center ice in what is widely considered to be the best goalie fight in NHL history. Colorado's Patrick Roy, thinking McCarty and Shanahan were about to double-team Foote, skated out of his crease to even things up. That's when Detroit's Mike Vernon came out to greet him. Despite being five inches shorter and weighing 23 pounds less than Roy, Vernon battered and bloodied his opponent.

While overtaxed medics immediately jumped over the boards to tend to Lemieux, the linesmen ushered the parade to the penalty box—but wondered what to do with McCarty. Both had turned to Devorski, saying almost simultaneously, "Dude, you're going to throw him out, right? McCarty's done, eh?"

"Nope," Devorski said without pausing to think about it. "He's staying in."

In fact, McCarty didn't even get the requisite five-minute fighting major. Instead, he was assessed a double-minor for roughing. And Lemieux? He wasn't penalized at all—not even a two-minute minor for refusing to fight back and getting his ass kicked.

"Believe me," Devorski said in a telephone interview more than two decades later, "if I could have assessed something like that, I would have."

But it was his explanation for not coming down harder on McCarty that was both astonishingly, refreshingly candid and sincere.

"My memory was, I just couldn't forget what happened to Kris Draper," Devorski said. "I'm getting ready for the game, and they're showing the highlights on TV—Draper's face after he got hit. I'm thinking, *Holy fuck*.

I'm being honest with you: McCarty should have been thrown out. He should have got 2-5-10 and game [misconduct] and be gone. But my gut told me, 'This guy [Lemieux] had it coming.' I wouldn't let it go. I couldn't. So I told the linesmen, 'No, I'm keeping him in the game.'"

Overall there were nine fights that night, all in the first two periods. While the Wings got the better of most of them—Foote and Roy were bloodied along with Lemieux—Detroit trailed 3-5 with less than twelve minutes to go before mounting a furious and unforgettable comeback.

Martin Lapointe scored his fourteenth of the season at 8:27 of the third with assists from Sergei Fedorov and Larry Murphy. And Brendan Shanahan tied just 36 seconds later with his forty-sixth goal, with assists from Igor Larionov and Jamie Pushor.

The Wings needed a hero in OT, and the guy who turned up to score the winning goal, by all retrospective accounts, should never have even been in the game. Larionov made the play with a spectacular move just across the blue line. He then passed to Shanahan, who one-timed the puck to McCarty breaking into the slot, and he redirected it past Roy from just outside the left post.

Game over.

Delirium overwhelmed the crowd of 19,983. At the other end, Mike Vernon celebrated the 300th victory of his career. And Devorski skated off the ice, thinking the last thing he needed was *that guy* to be the hero.

"Yeah, overtime, then Darren McCarty sticks it up my ass by scoring the winning goal," Devorski said. "I knew there would be some, uh, discussion about that afterward. Every time I see that goal—it's on TV all the time, eh?—I'm thinking, *Oh shit*.

Bottom line, though? Everybody knows paybacks are a bitch, eh?"

Right or wrong, many hockey lifers of a certain age saw nothing amiss with Devorski's call given the way justice was long administered in the NHL. But he knows a referee in today's game would never survive a decision like that.

"I can tell you this," Devorski said, "if I made that call today, I'd get fired on the spot."

And therein lies the difference between the kind of hockey many of us loved—and miss desperately—and today's game administered by Green Peace and assorted other pacifists who are running it into a slushy ditch.

———————●———————

There's a postscript to this story, again told by Devorski: On retiring as a referee, Devorski was elevated by the league to serve as a supervisor of officials, essentially monitoring the games, grading refs and linesmen on their performance, and offering guidance on how they might improve.

One assignment, during the COVID-19 pandemic when teams were playing to empty, cavernous arenas, took Devorski to Detroit. He typically would be assigned a perch in the press box, far above the ice surface. On this night, though, he found a comfortable spot a bit lower. It happened to be the section where Red Wings alumni congregate when they attend games.

"So I'm sitting there, watching the game, and all of a sudden this guy walks in—the place is empty, right?—and sits about five seats away from me," Devorski said. "I look over, and it's Darren McCarty."

McCarty looked over too and recognized the former ref.

"The period ends, and Darren comes over to me and wraps his arms around me, giving me a great big hug," Devorski said. "And he says, 'I love you, man. Thank you. Thank you.'"

And now, finally, you know the rest of the story.

The Precious
Metals Exchange

In the late 1980s, when National Hockey League teams began drafting the top Soviet players and it became increasingly clear that the Iron Curtain was beginning to rust and crack, Red Army Club and National Team coach Viktor Tikhonov was frequently asked about his players one day playing for that big silver trophy awarded to the NHL champion each year.

Tikhonov had a stock response, albeit a bit snarky: "Our players," he would say, "prefer to dream of gold, not silver."

Eventually, however, his players began to experience firsthand the difference between playing for gold in the Olympics and other world competitions—and the Stanley Cup. It was profound, and sometimes even shocking, when some of the game's most decorated players—men like Slava Fetisov and Igor Larionov, who simply were not accustomed to losing—wound up on the wrong side.

Igor Larionov explains:

Well, it took us—and I'm talking about the Russian players—some time to understand the significance of winning the Stanley Cup. I don't think you can compare it to any other trophy. I have won a lot playing for Soviet Union teams. When you're raised in the Soviet system, you play for gold medals; you play for championships in Olympics, World Championships, Canada Cups. But those are short tournaments—maximum two weeks. And so for us, you know, basically you can decide the gold medal in three games after the preliminary round—quarterfinals, semifinals and finals.

So basically, it's three Game 7s right there. But in the Stanley Cup playoffs, it's a grind, a marathon. And it's *after* an 82-game season. Then the playoffs, best-of-seven series, four rounds. And the adversity you go through, you have to psychologically be ready to show up every night. You win one game and it really doesn't mean anything because there is a mad team that you're going to have to play the next night again and the next night again and all over again to maybe seven games.

But it is not done yet. It is only one round. Then you have to go to the second round, and that is a tough grind, mentally and physically. You have to have stamina and character and also the desire to go out and do your best every single night, every shift.

And at the end, when you win the Cup, you realize, you know this is like a huge accomplishment. You reach the summit with a group of players, and with management, and with all the fans who were with you from the first day.

So, of course, I would say this is the hardest trophy, by far, in my collection.

Here We Go Again

For the second time in three years, the Red Wings had earned a trip to the Stanley Cup Finals, but this time things were different. Dramatically different.

This time, no one was taking anything for granted. Unlike 1995, when the Wings rolled into the Finals against New Jersey with a 12-2 record in the first three rounds, Detroit was not the overwhelming favorite. This time, the Legion of Doom-led Philadelphia Flyers, captained by MVP Eric Lindros, were the oddsmakers' sweethearts.

Few except for a couple of homers among the media in Detroit (guilty) gave the Red Wings much of a chance to end a Stanley Cup drought of more than four decades.

And then they dropped the puck.

Here's Kris Draper:

All I remember is that when we got to the Stanley Cup Finals, everyone was talking about the size and strength and speed of the Philadelphia Flyers. And everyone was questioning Detroit, once again, with so many Europeans. Are we too small? Yeah, we're fast and we're a puck-possession team, but we're not strong enough to get the puck from Philadelphia.

The one thing I know is that there was a lot of build-up about Vladimir Konstantinov going up against the Legion of Doom led by Eric Lindros. And of course, Scotty being Scotty, who starts Game 1 of the Stanley Cup Finals against that line? It's the Grind Line and it's Nick Lidstrom and Larry Murphy on defense.

To me it's just amazing how Scotty was going to match up—especially with those two defensemen—who could help control the puck with that first good pass. He was going to

use three different lines to go against their big line, all different. That was something no other team could do. You could throw out a Steve Yzerman-led line with the way he plays. And you want to play physical. How about Brendan Shanahan and Marty Lapointe? There it is. You want to play physical against the Grind Line? We can do that too.

And talk about puck possession? You throw out Igor, Sergei, and Kozzie over the boards as well. That was the one thing that really stood out for me, how Scotty kind of . . . Everyone was thinking one thing, and of course Scotty does the other thing.

We came into Philadelphia and we were able to win Game 1. We scored right off the bat with a big shorthanded goal. Malts [Kirk Maltby] ended up scoring that goal. That was so important for our hockey club because you listen and read all that stuff people were saying, it's just human nature [to doubt]. Then you line up against these guys and they were big and strong, you know? But we were a pretty good hockey team ourselves.

When you look at the players that we had, it's amazing that when people talked about us they thought that we were too European or too soft. We had Joe Kocur. We had Darren McCarty. We had Kirk

Maltby, Brendan Shanahan, and Marty LaPointe. And we had Vladimir Konstantinov.

Those guys, they were big guys who could play any style of hockey. But you know that one hit, the one on Dale Hawerchuk at Joe Louis Arena at center ice? That was probably one of the hardest hits I'd ever seen. And I'd say it was just a bit of a statement: "You know what? We can play hard too. Want to play physical? We can play physical too."

To me, that was just Vladimir Konstantinov evolving as one of the young, up-and-coming defensemen in the game. And we were seeing it happen right then. Vladdie was just outstanding all playoffs for us. His compete was just off the charts.

What's Gordie Doing There?

*Dave Lewis had the floor. Actually, he had the whole house. But
we were in his lovely suburban Detroit home, on the lower level, a
tricked-out man cave with all manner of photos, memorabilia, and
framed sweaters that paid tribute to the guy who played more than
1,000 games as an NHL defenseman and then worked behind the
bench as a coach for nearly double that number.*

*Among the framed items was a poster featuring a poem he had writ-
ten to inspire his team heading into the Stanley Cup tournament in
1998, Sixteen for Sixteen.*

*But at that moment in his home, Lewis was on a roll. And then
he hits us with this:*

"Do you have time for another story?"

Uh, do we ever!

*Turns out, Dave Lewis is the equal of Brendan Shanahan when
it comes to spinning a good yarn.*

As Lewis tells it:

Okay, it's Game 3 of the Stanley Cup Finals. The year is 1997, and the Red Wings are playing Philadelphia. Joe Louis is alive. It's got a heartbeat. It's pulsating. In the locker room before the game, you could hear the people stamping their feet in the stands. There was unbelievable excitement, unbelievable pressure to win, unbelievable nerves.

And our team was focused, but you could sense with the players that there was a nervousness about them. So now we get on the bench; the National Anthem is done; it's over. The fans settle into their seats. And then—I'll never forget this. The puck is dropped. It's Eric Lindros against Steve Yzerman on the opening face-off.

I'm watching for a matchup. Vladimir Konstantinov is not on the ice now, but he's going to go next. But as soon as the puck is dropped, Scotty Bowman taps me on the shoulder.

"Dave?"

"What, Scotty?"

"Look across by the penalty box over there. Isn't that Gordie Howe?"

"What?"

"Look. Is that Gordie Howe?"

The game is going on now. It's started. I'm trying to watch the play, but Scotty is pointing across the ice asking me if that was Gordie Howe over there.

And I said, "Yeah, that's Gordie Howe, but I can't tell who he's with."

And Scotty says, "How's he going to enjoy the game sitting there?"

"Scotty, I don't know!"

I'm a nervous wreck, the players are a nervous wreck, and now Scotty points up to the Ilitches' suite and says, "Don't you think Gordie should be sitting up there? Look up there. They've got a lot of people up there, but there's room for him."

So our players are hearing all of this too and wondering what's going on. But I actually think they're calming down. This was during the first and second shifts of that game. And our players actually said, they're all looking at Scotty like, "What are you talking about? The game is on! It's Game 3 of the Finals; we've gotta win this thing!"

So this conversation, to me, it felt like five minutes, but it was probably like 40 seconds—through at least one rotation. But the players calmed down, and the rest is history.

That was just amazing to me. Scotty knew exactly what he was doing. I'm going, like, "What are you doing?" Barry [Smith] was nervous; the players were nervous. It was our first game back in Detroit and we've got a chance. But if we lose, it's 2-1, and you don't know what's going to happen. But that's Scotty Bowman. He knew what we all needed.

But, oh boy, the anticipation of us coming back to Detroit after winning Game 1 and Game 2 was incredible. I remember driving to Joe Louis Arena early, getting ready to go to the game. And there were people with brooms sticking out of their cars; people dancing in the back of pick-up trucks. It seemed like all the bars were full. You couldn't get a ticket to the game.

Then I'll never forget Game 4, that final thirty seconds. The Flyers scored to make it 2-1. And I'm on the bench thinking, *Oh my God!* Like Scotty always says, anything can happen in hockey. I'm thinking, *Let's get out of these last twenty seconds and win our Cup because we don't want to go back to Philadelphia 3-1.*

As it turned out, we won, and the place erupted. The fans partied for a week. It was incredible. A generational thing. And the players were exhausted and relieved. You couldn't move in the locker room because our families and all our close personal friends were in there.

It was amazing. It really was a special time.

The Longest Seconds

Ask any player or coach who's been through it, and nothing lasts longer than the final seconds of the final game of the season. The game you've dreamt your whole life of winning. The one you know you're going to win, but only if you can keep the other frantically furious team from scoring, tying it up, sending it into overtime when anything can happen.

For Detroit players on the bench in the final seconds of Game 4 at the Joe on June 7, 1997, it was like the bored high-school student watching the clock seem to tick backward during algebra class. They would follow the action on the ice, then look up at the clock— always amazed that so few seconds had ticked away.

For players on the ice, it was even more nerve-wracking. At a critical moment, the Red Wings desperately needed a hero—and he showed up just in time. Guess who?

Nicklas Lidstrom remembers:

I was actually on the ice with Vladdie in those last seconds before the buzzer. I remember we were up 2-0 and they scored. There could have been about ten seconds left [actually fifteen] when they made it 2-1.

All of a sudden, this is a game again. If they get another one, it's going to overtime. I remember those last winding seconds: the puck is behind our net and I see Vladdie falling on the puck on purpose, then waiting and waiting for the buzzer while Vladdie just keeps the puck there, beneath him. Then that feeling when the buzzer *finally* goes off. Mike Vernon is raising his hands in the net.

And Vladdie is still lying there with the puck and you see the arena just go crazy. It's hard to, you know, talk about, to put into words. It was such a tremendous feeling.

It was such a relief after losing in the finals in '95, then winning 62 games in '96 and not winning the Cup. Then, in '97, it finally happened for us.

Like a Live Grenade

*Red Wings fans of a certain age can describe in vivid detail their
own everlasting memory of the final frenetic seconds ticking off in
Game 4 of the 1997 Stanley Cup Finals: Goalie Mike Vernon
tossing his stick in the air as he raised both arms over his head; his
teammates littering the ice with all manner of sticks and gloves as
they raced toward the goalie for a victorious scrum; more teammates
streaming over the boards to join them; coaches behind the Detroit
bench embracing; the Philadelphia Flyers, who seconds before
threatened to tie the game with what seemed like a team meeting
around the crease, skating dejectedly toward their bench.*

*Dave Lewis remembers all that, but the final scene he'll forever
remember is of Vladimir Konstantinov lying in the corner, shield-
ing the puck from anyone who dared jab him in the ribs with their
sticks to set it free for one more shot at the Detroit goal, hoping to
extend that series.*

Here's how it plays out in Lewis's mind's eye:

It's the final game of the Stanley Cup Finals in Joe Louis Arena, and
there's a few seconds left. The puck goes into his corner, and the next

thing you know, it looks like he's lying on it. He's trying to protect it, and it's impossible for the other team to even touch the puck, let alone try to get it past Mike Vernon at the time.

Vladimir Konstantinov played until the game was over. If there had been someone in the corner to hit, he would have gone into the corner to hit him. He would have kept going, doing anything he had to do, until the clock ended. And he got to carry the Stanley Cup that night.

And I'll never forget that either, Vladimir Konstantinov with the Cup. I don't know what it weighs, but it's not light [actually, 34.5 pounds]. And he's throwing it around like a paper doll.

He really understood what he, individually, and the team, collectively, went through to win it. And I think that was the passion and joy—and the relief—when you see that from a player like that. Just throwing that Cup into the air.

He accomplished the dream of a lifetime. Well, I don't know if that was his dream when he was younger, but I know it was a dream for him once he came over here. It was the experience of a lifetime and you know, sadly, that was the last time he got to pump it over his head as an athlete.

But the emotion he showed that night was fierce. Just fierce.

The After-Party

Well past midnight, while thousands in the streets still celebrated the first Stanley Cup championship in Detroit in 42 years, Steve Yzerman tucked the big trophy gently into the narrow confines of his Porsche and rode off.

The party was on. First stop, Big Daddy's restaurant, the unofficial team hangout on Woodward Avenue, north of Detroit. But as it turned out, they were too pooped to party.

•————————————•

Brendan Shanahan remembers:

Later on that night we went to a bar restaurant and it was private, just us and our families. Kris Draper still had his equipment on. He didn't even take it off before he went out.

But one of my favorite moments was when, maybe an hour, hour and a half into this party, the Cup is there and our family members and close friends are all partying with it, and there was just this moment when I guess the adrenalin and the high that we had from the game, and the physical toll that the entire playoffs had taken, just sort of hit us.

It was this great scene where I saw family members, brothers, sisters, parents, friends, all drinking from the Cup and hooting and hollering. And then in the background I saw most of my teammates just scattered in chairs, maybe with a beer in their hands, Kris Draper with his equipment still on, all of us just sitting there sort of sweaty, tired, drained, but with these silly little grins on our faces.

We were all just leaning back and watching our family members play with the trophy that we all dreamed of winning. And you know, it was a great feeling, that first night. It was a relief for many of us. We only had two guys on that team who had ever won a Stanley Cup—Mike Vernon [with Calgary in 1989] and Joe Kocur [with the New York Rangers in 1994].

And now the rest of us were Stanley Cup champions, and we just felt relief.

Finally

When they interviewed him for the general manager's job shortly after buying the Red Wings from the Norris family in 1982, Mike and Marian Ilitch asked Jim Devellano how long it would take to win the Stanley Cup. In typical Devellano fashion, he didn't hesitate and he didn't mince words.

"Eight years," he said.

Marian was shocked. Why so long? she wondered.

"If you want to do it right, like we built the Islanders in New York through the draft, it'll take at least that long," he told them.

At least.

It wound up taking fifteen years, and Devellano has counted his blessings ever since that he was around long enough to see it. His tenure as GM lasted about eight years before he was replaced by Bryan Murray and elevated to the position of senior vice president.

While he had a few near misses on the firing line—Marian always came to his defense—Devellano remains with the organization

40 years after that memorable dinner. That makes him the lon-gest-serving employee in the history of the franchise, by far.

———————●———————

Here's Jimmy Devellano:

Stanley Cups—you don't win them often, and when you do it means a lot. We had a parade downtown with 1.2 million people. They had poured their hearts out for that team, and it meant a lot to them too. It had been a long time.

It was a total relief for me because I really thought we would get it done quicker. I first said eight years, and when it doesn't happen you start to make changes—managers, coaches, players. But while you're a little disappointed that you haven't been able to get it all together, to be fair we really did have some good teams prior to the Cups.

Of course, you're measured by winning championships. I still remember how it felt. It was fabulous.

I know when Steve Yzerman got the Stanley Cup from Gary Bettman, it certainly was a relief for Steve. He had been maligned a little bit for not being able to win. Remember, it was Steve's fourteenth year, and he'd been through a lot. The organization had been through a lot because it had disappointed too often.

So when he finally had the Cup, he made a tremendous symbolic gesture. He handed it off to Slava Fetisov and Igor Larionov, the two old Russians. That was recognition from a North American, a Canadian, to two Russians, saying, "Hey, without you guys, without your play and your leadership, without you guys prodding the younger Russians, we wouldn't have done it."

That was Steve Yzerman's way of saying how much those guys were a big part of that '97 Cup win.

You know, when you have great players, other players watch and see how they do it. They try to copy when they see it's the right way to play the game. They learned. Remember, it wasn't always the Russian Five. Scotty would break them up and the North Americans would play with them, and they would learn to play that way as well. Now, of course we already had two non-Russians who could play the Russian style. Yzerman could, and certainly Nick Lidstrom, so we had two other great superstars who could adapt and play that way.

And when you put average players with real good players, they can improve a little bit too. That had repercussions throughout our league. When the NHL under John Ziegler decided they were going for a bigger footprint across the United States, and go from a 21-team league to 30, that's a big expansion and it could never, ever have been accomplished without European-born players.

The Russians were a big, big part of it. I was here. I knew what the player personnel was like across the league. You couldn't go from 21 to 30 teams without the Europeans who were able to come over here and make our league stronger. And the Russians did it, big time.

'It's Really Hard'

Certainly, it took him awhile, but from the time he was drafted in 1983 to when he departed to take the general manager's job in Tampa Bay in 2010, Steve Yzerman had spent twenty-seven years with the Detroit Red Wings. In that time, they won four Stanley Cups—roughly one every eight years.

That's not a bad batting average, considering that each season begins now with 32 teams all with the same objective.

But few people on the planet understand and appreciate the challenge of winning the Stanley Cup, as a player and as an executive, more than Steve Yzerman. It was he, after all, who built the framework of that Tampa team that won back-to-back championships in 2020-21.

And now he's back in Hockeytown, trying to bring home another Stanley Cup.

Here's The Captain:

I was on some really, really good teams that didn't win, you know? It's just incredibly difficult from a player's perspective, from an organization's perspective. It's really hard to win. So many things have to go well. You're competing against all the other teams who have the exact same goal and who are trying every bit as hard as you are.

And you're dealing with human beings, athletes who get injured. A lot of things can happen to derail the best-laid plans. So it can become really difficult, and even more so in today's NHL because of the salary cap. Sometimes you're forced to make decisions based on not necessarily what's most competitive but on the salary cap. That's the system we all deal with.

It's an incredibly difficult trophy to win as a player, with the grind of training camp, the regular season, then getting into the playoffs and having to, for two months, go through the ups and downs and just find the energy to perform at your best every single game, playing well, staying calm, and conserving your energy.

Then, when it goes south on you, because it always goes south at some point, not completely falling apart, being able to recover from a mistake, or an upset, or a tough loss, and coming back the next night and playing. That's the hardest part of it all, that two-month stretch. It's exhausting, really a mental challenge.

For me, what I learned from the whole experience, that period or that era in Red Wings hockey, was about a group of guys with strong leadership from above, with specific direction, given a task and everyone buying into it and putting the goal ahead of everything else. It was about putting all egos aside and really enjoying the whole process, understanding what the goal was and sticking to that.

And we accomplished what we wanted to accomplish. It was a

special group of guys, various personalities from all over the world, and it became about winning. That was the Ilitches' mandate and Scotty Bowman's mandate, and we as a group—it's hard to replicate that—but we were able to do it. From my perspective, it was a really special time and a really enjoyable time because we had a really tremendous team.

A bunch of those guys are in the Hall of Fame, but when you walked into that locker room, you were just one of the bunch. You played, and you played to win. When Scotty tapped you on the shoulder, whether you were playing right wing or left wing or defense, you went over the boards and did your best. Those were the greatest years of my playing career. One, because we won, obviously. But, boy, the entire process was a lot of fun.

The Wrong Damned Glass

*Sometime between the after-party at Big Daddy's and the parade—
two decades later it remained a blur even for Dave Lewis—he and
his fellow assistant coach, Barry Smith, and their wives were
invited to the Konstantinovs' home for a traditional Russian celebration. The Larionovs were there as well.*

*And then, just as Vladimir was about to propose a toast, a tradition
cherished by Russians, calamity ensued.*

———•————————•———

Dave Lewis picks up the story:

So we're down in the basement, and Vladimir has a real nice wine
shelf and a bar down there. And he opened the wine and poured it
into a water glass. Well, two minutes later, Igor comes down and he looks
at the glasses and just starts screaming at Vladdie in Russian.

Igor takes the wine and pours it down the sink. Now it could have
been a hundred-dollar bottle of wine, but Igor didn't care. He gets out
the proper wine glasses—and he's still yelling at poor Vladdie, who probably couldn't care less what kind of glass you're drinking wine out of. It
didn't matter to me either. But it sure did matter to Igor.

I just thought it was funny, but that's Igor. Very refined. He introduced chess to the team. He had wine selections for the guys instead of Labatt's Blue. And he had his mannerisms. That's where he got the nickname "Professor."

He *looked* like a professor. He talked politics—and we talked about not bringing politics into the locker room. But I remember he didn't want to go to the White House after one of the Cups because of the leadership of the country and what was going on internationally. That was a bit unheard of, by hockey standards anyway. But Igor was like that. He brought a worldly vision and experience to the rink every day.

A Sobering Gut Punch

*The party didn't last long—no thanks to that pot-smoking jerk
masquerading as a limo driver who fell asleep at the wheel and
crashed into a tree. Three Russian team members in the rear of
the limo were seriously injured, two of them critically. It was an
unspeakable, mind-numbing moment for those who had endured
more than four decades of frustration and disappointment.*

*"For us, and probably for the whole city of Detroit and Red Wings
fans, winning the Stanley Cup was life or death," Steve Yzerman
said. "A week later we realized the Cup isn't life or death, you
know? If there's anything we learned from the accident, it was,
'Hey let's keep all this hockey in perspective.' It certainly put everything in perspective for us."*

Here's Dave Lewis:

The worst part was, you worked so hard to win a Stanley Cup. Now
you're at the pinnacle of your professional career, emotionally.
You're with your families, and they know the sacrifices you've gone

through—not just this year, but since you were a young child. Your parents, your aunts, your uncles, your former teammates.

The city, the state was electrified by the Red Wings winning a Stanley Cup for the first time in so long, and it was a party from day one. And then the accident happened. I found out about it from somebody in New York. I was in bed already because we were exhausted, you know, from all the celebrations, and he said there was a car accident. I said, "What are you talking about?" I hadn't heard about anything. He said, "You'd better call somebody. I think some of your players were in a limo that got in an accident."

And sure enough, the next thing you know everybody was at the hospital. They just stopped doing whatever they were doing that night and went. And it was . . . it was just devastating for Vladdie and Sergei Mnatsakanov—for their families, and for their careers.

It just doesn't seem right, because they did everything right, everything they were supposed to do. They had a limousine. They got in the vehicle and they were being transported from a golf outing. It just shouldn't happen like that. Vladdie lost God's gift to play hockey. He survived but, you know, it's just difficult to think about.

I remember going to the hospital right after the accident. He was on a respirator making things function for him, keeping him alive. And we all hoped that his fighting spirit that he showed us on the ice would transfer in the hospital. And sure enough, it did. I'm not a doctor, but I'm sure it had an influence on him surviving such a traumatic injury.

I visited him in Florida with John Wharton and Dougie Brown. We flew down when he was in therapy, still fighting.

But that accident shortened our celebration to five or six days, whatever it was. And for the rest of the summer—we did get the Stanley Cup, all of us, but it wasn't the way it was supposed to be.

I'll never forget this as a coach, how our players quietly decided that they were going to win the Stanley Cup next year for Vladimir Konstantinov and Sergei Mnatsakanov. I don't know if anybody physically said it out loud, if it came out of their voices, but it certainly permeated through that group of players.

As a coach I knew that it was going to happen. I felt it, and I'm sure the players did too. If you asked them, they'd probably say the same thing. It's very difficult to win, especially back to back because you're exhausted, but they were going to win it again.

I think the only release the players had in the locker room that season was when they stepped on the ice. Then they got to do what they love, and what they did best: play hockey. That's what Vladdie did. They all knew the kind of warrior he was, and now there's just an empty locker. On the ice, that was their away time from thinking about the accident. They couldn't do that when they got on the ice, so that was their release.

And it brought it to a point in the playoffs where they knew that this was what they had to do. There was no denying them. Regardless of opponent, regardless of situation, regardless of the city, regardless of injury. Collectively, the team knew it had to do this for Vladimir Konstantinov and Sergei Mnatsakanov. They were on a mission.

For me, and I think for the players too, the realization that we were that close was when they showed Vladimir Konstantinov on the Jumbotron over center ice in Washington during Game 4. Then it really set in—I think even for the opponent that night.

It starts with the players in Washington and the management, what respect they had for Vladimir Konstantinov, and then it permeated out into the fans. They knew what kind of player he was, what kind of warrior he was. And it shows the class that they had at that time to give him that ovation, to give him that respect. Knowing the circumstances of the accident, of the tragedy, of his family, and that meant a lot, I think, to him and everyone involved with the Red Wings.

It took the story out of Detroit. It took it to a national audience on TV, both in the U.S. and in Canada. It changed the focus from competing for the Stanley Cup to appreciating a wounded athlete who will never, ever play again. And that sort of showed everybody what fans are made of, what hockey fans are made of anyway—that they don't just cheer for one person or one team; they cheer for the sport and the athletes in the sport.

And finally, the presentation of the Cup. I'll never forget this: the Zamboni doors open, and out comes Vladimir Konstantinov, with Slava Fetisov pushing him. He had a big smile on his face, and there were probably bigger smiles on every player's face. And the Cup didn't matter to them as much as they just wanted to give it to him so they could relay the message of, "We did this for you. All our passion, all our love for you. All our experiences this year were for you. You were the focus. You were our focal point. And we're glad to say this all happened because of you. You're one of us, and you'll always be one of us."

That's certainly what I felt. The crowd, I can't even remember if they stayed or if they left. I don't remember anything. I just remember the emotion of that transfer, of Stevie putting it on his lap and him having the Cup. It was like another one of those life moments that you'll never forget. All that emotion. It's so hard to win the Stanley Cup, and when you win it, you're emotionally spent and drained.

But there was an added—not incentive, that's not the right word. There was an added piece of everyone's soul going into the process to give the Cup to your teammate. And Slava Fetisov, if there are tears coming from his eyes, he's not crying because he's not a man or he's not courageous. He's crying out of passion and joy of the experience that they all lived through to give Vladimir this Cup.

Nobody knows what it's like to go back to your hotel room after taking a slapshot off the ankle and the pain is so intense that you can't sleep at night, but you have to go to practice the next day and play the next night. Nobody knows that except the athletes. Vladimir Konstantinov knew all about that. The players he played with knew the pain and suffering he went through to win that Cup in '97.

Those are some of the things that you only experience as part of that group in that locker room—and that's what they were giving back. All the pain, all the suffering, all the sacrifice is *for you*. And it made them feel better than it probably made Vladdie feel by getting it.

There are certain things in in life you don't forget, and this is one of them I'll never forget. Vladdie couldn't hoist it above his head, but he certainly knew what it meant—and who he got it from. But most important of all, he was there. He was with us. And it . . . it was just perfect.

Believe

After bringing the Stanley Cup back to Detroit for the first time in 42 years, the Red Wings had every right to kick back and feel good about their hard-fought success. But no.

Not after a limo crash ended a celebration that didn't even last a week. Not after losing two beloved team members to catastrophic injuries. No, not on their watch. That much was certain, though also unspoken, even as they rode their bus north and across the state to their first-ever training camp in Traverse City, the Lake Michigan resort town.

But no one was thinking much about golfing on some of the finest courses in the country or chartering a boat for some salmon fishing on Grand Traverse Bay in the leisure hours when they weren't playing hockey. No. Not then.

This team meant business, and this was just the first business trip of the new season.

Brendan Shanahan remembers:

I think going into the next season we were even more determined. We wanted to prove to people that we were for real, that it wasn't a fluke.

And obviously certain people stepped up in Vladdie's absence. Nick Lidstrom was always a great defensemen, but I think he became an even greater defensemen. Whether he just decided he was going to bring more or maybe it was just the assignments that Vladdie always took were now Nick's, but Nick all of a sudden went on a run of winning Norris Trophies.

I remember having a conversation with Steve during the playoffs early on. I don't know where we were, somewhere warm, maybe Arizona, and I just remember saying to him at lunch, "I feel like we're even more determined than we were last year." And he agreed. We had this anger about us, an anger mixed with determination that we were going to win this again.

Every time we'd lose a game, someone would write, "Well, they're complacent; they're not as good as last year." And that would just piss us off even more. I just remember all of us feeling this real driven anger to win it again.

We all hoped Vladdie was going to improve. We thought he'd be coming back at some point. We all thought, you know, that we were just minding the shop so to speak while he was rehabilitating. And we had this BELIEVE patch put on our shoulder, but it wasn't just for Vladdie. It was also for [massage therapist] Sergei Mnatsakanov, who was also loved, *loved* by all the guys in our room. He was just a special, special man.

Slava [Fetisov] was still on our team too. We all knew it was Slava's last year, and I think we all just took it as a personal challenge to make sure it ended right. And it did.

Survivor's Guilt

Credit Dave Lewis, with an assist from Slava Kozlov, for the iconic "Believe" logo that inspired a team and its legion of fans entering the encore 1997-98 season.

It began with a rock, painted with the word "Believe," that Slava Kozlov placed on the upper shelf of Vladimir Konstantinov's locker. It was a gift from a fan, he said. Lewis took it a step further, conceiving a patch with the word in both languages, BELIEVE/VERIM ("We believe"), and the initials of both critically injured teammates: VK/SM for Vladdie and Sergei Mnatsanakov.

An iconic symbol to be sure, though the players who remained in that Detroit dressing room didn't need it. They had an even stronger visual that inspired them every day throughout that season and beyond.

Kris Draper explains:

I remember the first game that we played the next season. Vladdie's jersey was hung up there in his locker, and as I'm getting dressed I check over my left shoulder and there was a rock there that had the word "Believe" on it.

It was just something that . . . it shouldn't have happened, and you just kept thinking about it, and it was hard. But you know, we're hockey players and we have to play hockey. It doesn't sound humane. It doesn't sound right. But the bottom line is, we had to play hockey. And we all just kind of felt like, "You know what? Let's just play as hard as we can, and do the things that we did, for Vladdie and Sergei." And as the season was going on, that's kind of truly how we all felt.

It was Dave Lewis who came up with that patch, and obviously we had to get clearance through the league to get that put on our uniforms. They [the NHL] were very supportive, and that's something that meant a lot to all of us; we were able to honor Sergei and Vladdie through everything that they were dealing with.

And here we are, showing up to the rink and playing. Like I said, there were some times when you just kind of, you felt guilty about what was going on, what they were going through. But the bottom line for us was that we all kind of dug down deep and got a little extra. And you know, this is an unbelievable sports town, a very supportive sports town, and everyone rallied around us and what was going on with the Detroit Red Wings.

It was an emotional year with everything that had gone on, a lot of the celebrations, raising the banner, getting the rings, having the Stanley Cup back at the Joe. But it was always bittersweet because of everything that happened just six days after we won the Cup.

And then we get to Game 4 of the Finals the next year, and we have Scotty Bowman coming in and reminding us that we have an opportunity to do it again. I'll tell you this: We weren't losing that hockey game. There was no chance with the emotions we were feeling that night and having Vladdie there.

I remember that one picture from the end zone, with Chris Osgood as he throws his arms up in the air, and you can kind of see the whole rink. And you know what? We did it. And probably one of the greatest memories that I have as a Stanley Cup champion and being there at center ice was when Stevie got the Cup and he gave it to Vladdie. It was something that meant so much to all of us to be able to do that. You know, when we say that we did it for Vladdie, I mean, *We did it for Vladdie.* And that was something that makes us all so proud.

Made for Hollywood

One of the most difficult challenges in professional sport—perhaps competition of every kind—is finding ways to reach peak performance even on nights when it's just not there.

Oh, it's easy for fans to say, "C'mon, you're being paid obscene amounts of money. Get out there and be the superstars you're supposed to be."

Manufacturing motivation—far easier said than done. Ask any athlete—especially one on a team coming off a championship season. The mission, incredibly difficult as it was, had finally been accomplished. Now you expect us to do it again? For many athletes the notion is exhausting even right out of the gate.

But the Detroit Red Wings had no such issues going into the 1997-98 season.

Steve Yzerman explains:

Well, after winning the Cup, going through everything the organization did over the course of the summer, we just showed up and I think it went without saying. It was like, "You know what? We're here to play. Let's just appreciate playing." Of course we wanted to win again. But it was very businesslike, a very professional attitude.

We showed up, and we just played. We knew what the expectation was from our coaching staff. It was a huge loss, not having Vladdie in the line-up, but we still felt we had a really good team. We didn't talk at all about the playoffs; we just went to work every day.

If there was anything we learned from the accident, it was to keep things in perspective. For us and probably for the whole city of Detroit and Red Wings fans, winning the Cup had felt like life or death. A week later we realized it wasn't life or death at all, you know? That put everything in perspective for us. We showed up, performed well, got into the playoffs—and were fortunate enough to win it again.

The motivation we had in that year was definitely unspoken, but it was there. And again, the accident put everything in our careers in perspective. And it allowed us, the good and the bad moving forward, to remind ourselves that we're playing a game. It didn't mean we didn't want to win as much or weren't willing to put the effort in, but it kept things in perspective and it allowed us to become even closer, more so than ever, and play for one common goal.

I know there was some added motivation, particularly as we got into the playoffs, to try to win. But we never ever discussed it. Not once was there ever, well, actually I believe Scotty Bowman, before Game 4 [of the Stanley Cup Finals], talked about the situation. Scotty didn't give a lot of speeches, but when he did, they were unbelievable.

There were a couple others that I don't need to talk about, but this one, he gave a speech about what's really important, and it was very impactful for our players. I wish I could have that as a recording because it meant a lot to all of us.

After the game, seeing Vladdie with that big smile on his face—he was really happy to be a part of it. And I know Igor [Larionov] and Slava [Fetisov] were really happy. Well, I don't know if "happy" is even the right word, but to have them, to have all the Russian guys there . . . We all loved Vladdie, but those guys had a special bond with him.

When Vladdie came out on the ice, everyone felt very, very good that he could be there and be a part of it. And we were able to give him the Stanley Cup. It's like, that's what movies are made of, you know?

It wasn't the thought at the time, but it kind of blew everybody away. And it was very emotional for us all, a bunch of guys; we're all athletes and kind of proud guys and we're not trying to show a lot of emotion or anything. But for us, inside, it was, uh, it was . . . something I hope I never have to experience again, or want to experience, but it was pretty amazing, that whole experience.

And you know, seeing Sergei now, and when we see Vladdie, we know what these guys were. We know what kind of athlete Vladdie was. We know Sergei Mnatsakanov was, is a special human being, beloved as well for his attitude, for his work ethic. Just a fabulous human being.

What those guys had to go through and what it did for our organization, for us as players to come back and win, and then be able to celebrate the Stanley Cup with Vladdie on the ice, you know, I think it gave him some joy. And I would say for the other Russian guys it had to be somewhat of, maybe, a moment of serenity for them.

A Climate Change
in the Cold War

It didn't hurt that all five former Soviet players who landed in Detroit in the 1990s came from the same program, or "school," as Sergei Fedorov likes to say. And his word is a far more accurate description of the system Russians have deployed for decades to develop some of the greatest performers the sport of hockey has ever seen.

Some, who won Olympic and World Championship gold with the Soviet National Team, were known more than the younger players who left for the NHL before gaining much fame. But all were alumni of the iconic Soviet Red Army Club (CSKA), a team even more dominant in its league than baseball's New York Yankees and the National Hockey League's Montreal Canadiens.

Detroit's red and white sweaters didn't hurt either.

Igor Larionov explains:

The Russian Five and the Detroit Red Wings, we got a big following back home in Russia, where we also wore the red uniform of the Russian "machine"—the Big Red Machine. So, yes, we had a lot of fans those years when all five of us were playing a key role with the Detroit Red Wings.

And then when we were winning the Cup, people were watching the games because it was televised back home at, like, three o'clock in the morning. That generated some huge interest to Russians because five of their members were playing for Detroit, and that meant a lot to us. The Detroit Red Wings were, you know, like the people's team outside of Russia.

It's hard to imagine, but in those years it was like, not a Cold War exactly, but I guess perhaps they were harsh years of politics with Russia because of all the stuff going on in Europe, Afghanistan, many other things.

But hockey players are brothers. It doesn't matter what passport you carry, what country you come from. You're playing for the team. And for all of us to get reunited in Detroit, you know, it was very important to have an opportunity to kind of restore the success we had in the past and help to bring that success to the young players we play with on the Detroit Red Wings.

You know, Slava [Fetisov] was 39 and I was 37. Winning the Stanley Cup at that age was special because, you know, when are you going to have this opportunity again to play at the highest level, with such great players—and still enjoy the game?

But you know what? When you play, the game of hockey is completely separate from politics. It wasn't like in the old days of the Soviet Union when we were playing against Canada, the USA, or Germany or the Swedes and we must show the might of the Soviet Union—how big we are, how powerful, and at any cost we have to win.

Now we are in North America and we are part of a group, you know. It's international. That's what's good about North America, about the

United States: you have the freedom to express yourself. You make yourself by your talent, by your work ethic, by being a part of the group.

And that's what we did, actually. We showed the world. But you have to have the chance, you have to *believe*, and you've got to work hard for that. It's not about promoting the lifestyle of Russia, the mighty Soviet Union.

It was all about showing how the people of Russia, they have a soul and they have a heart. We showed that we're all the same; we just speak a different language and we were brought up in a different system. It opened up, it introduced the Russian culture, let's put it that way, by playing the game and then talking with the media—and to share this kind of skill with North American players.

It all comes from culture, the rich culture of Russia where we're always talking about poets and architecture and things that happened in the rich history of Russia. So we all come from that part of the world and we show that we're the same as you guys [Americans]. We just come from a different place.

But you know, we're willing to share, willing to make life better, the hockey better. That's what we tried to do. And if you touch anybody, their souls, their hearts, that's the goal. There's no politics. No propaganda. Just communicate and socialize and help to make life better.

A Special Ending

Fast-forward a few years following Detroit's back-to-back Stanley Cup titles in 1997-98. From the mid 1990s through a few years into the new millennium, four teams dominated the NHL.

Dallas was every bit the equal of Detroit and Colorado in the Western Conference. In fact, the Red Wings-Stars matchup in 1998 was by far the best series in that Stanley Cup tournament. The Stars would get their Cup in 1999 and reached the Finals again the following year, only to lose an epic battle with New Jersey—which dominated the Eastern Conference for nearly a decade, starting with that sweep of Detroit in the 1995 Finals.

New Jersey reached the Finals again in 2001, bowing to Colorado in a seven-game series. But the Red Wings, embarrassed by the stunning first-round elimination by Anaheim—in a four-game sweep, no less—would soon fix that in no uncertain terms.

In the waning years of the pre-salary-cap era in the NHL, when teams could simply throw money at their roster issues and make upgrades where needed, General Manager Ken Holland, armed with the Ilitches' checkbook, did just that. He was forced to fill a glaring vacancy with the loss of Vladimir Konstantinov and made a bold move by trading for Chris Chelios. But it was costly. Detroit sent two first-round draft picks and a young defenseman to Chicago in that deal.

Holland knew the team needed more offense, so he signed Brett Hull and Luc Robitaille. He also decided that with a roster like that, the Wings weren't going to be outplayed in goal, so he made a deal with Buffalo for Dominik Hasek. Included in Detroit's package to the Sabres was Slava Kozlov. With Konstantinov's career ended in the limo crash in 1997 and Slava Fetisov's retirement a year later, the Russian Five were down to two: Sergei Fedorov and Igor Larionov.

Clearly Holland was comfortably entrenched in the role he had assumed in the summer of 1997. And with these moves, he had pieced together a formidable roster—one of the most talented ever assembled in NHL history. Hasek, Hull, and Robitaille would join Chelios, Fedorov, Larionov, Nicklas Lidstrom, Brendan Shanahan, and Steve Yzerman. All were destined to become Honored Members of the Hockey Hall of Fame. So was Pavel Datsyuk, who was a rookie that season.

It was enough to convince Scotty Bowman—the architect of the roster that had won the two previous Cups—to return for one more season. How could he not? As Senior VP Jim Devellano likes to say, "If there's one thing Scotty loves, it's great hockey players."

Now he had a roster full of them, and he knew how to coach them. The Wings cruised to their third President's Trophy in eight seasons, then beat Vancouver and St. Louis in the first two rounds before encountering their only serious challenge in the playoffs. Colorado took them to seven games before the Wings advanced to face the Carolina Hurricanes in the Finals, a series that featured an interesting storyline.

The teams were owned by prominent Detroit business leaders whose hockey rivalry dated back decades when the youth teams they sponsored—the Ilitch family's Little Caesars, and Pete Karmanos's Compuware—battled for supremacy at nearly every age level in Michigan and Ontario. But with the Stanley Cup on the line, it was a mismatch, and the Red Wings were able to give Bowman the best of all parting gifts.

Kris Draper explains:

It's easy now to sit back and say that Scotty Bowman was a genius, the way he coached and how he got the most out of his players. Yes, he surrounded himself with players that he felt that he could win with, but it still wasn't easy—for anybody.

There were times when he'd challenge you. He wanted to see how you'd respond, and if you responded in a positive way, he truly appreciated that. I know for a fact how grateful he was after we won in 2002. He came around to everybody in the locker room and told them he was retiring, and he thanked them.

I remember when he came over and shook my hand, he said, "I'm done. I'm going to retire." It was emotional. You know, I had ten years with Scotty, and it was special. He made me a better hockey player and he made me a better person with the way that he challenged me. There were some times when it was hard and it was frustrating, but in the end I was a part of winning three Stanley Cups with Scotty Bowman and the Detroit Red Wings.

We were able to let him go out on top, and that's obviously something that any coach or any athlete would love to do. That was special.

We Are Family?

To retire No. 91 or not to retire it remains one of the most intense debates among Red Wings fans, however lopsided it may be. Take a poll and the numbers are overwhelmingly in favor of bestowing that honor on a three-time Stanley Cup champion—and the lone Hart Trophy winner as the NHL's most valuable player since Gordie Howe won his fourth and final one in 1963.

But the only votes that count are those cast by the Ilitch ownership family, and the prevailing thinking is that so long as the matriarch of the clan is with us, Sergei Fedorov's number will remain in moth balls.

To those who have earned her confidence, Marian Ilitch has made no secret of her feelings after the organization went to such lengths, at such expense, to orchestrate Fedorov's defection from the Soviet Union. And the owners who paid him so handsomely and were prepared to reward him with a contract that would have made him the highest-paid player in club history felt betrayed when he left $10 million on the table to sign with Anaheim in 2003.

The Ilitches felt like they treated Sergei Fedorov like a son. It's frankly how they've felt about every player who wore the sweater since they bought the team in 1982. And he turned his back on them.

Clearly, Fedorov would be elated by a change of heart. Listen between the lines of his words whenever the subject arises—it comes up in every trip he makes back to his second home in Detroit—and it's clear that he regrets his decision to leave. He tries to joke about getting bad advice from his agents, but perhaps that's not a joke.

However it happened, Fedorov's career began a fairly rapid descent after he left the Wings. Five games into his second season with the Mighty Ducks, he was traded to Columbus. In his third mediocre season with the Bluejackets, he was dispatched in another trade to Washington, where he spent less than a season and a half. He played his final NHL game in 1989, then closed his professional career with three seasons in Russia's Kontinental Hockey League.

So bottom line: Will it ever happen? Will we see No. 91 in the rafters one day?

Yes, and probably sooner than later—if only because that same Wings ownership knows it can recoup some much-needed goodwill among its fanbase. Not to mention packing Little Caesars Arena to those very same rafters with a ceremony honoring one of the franchise's all-time best players. After all, a full house is awfully rare for a rebuilding club—even in Hockeytown.

But for now, don't condemn ownership for dragging its feet on this decision. Money matters. And when you have enough to buy your own NHL franchise, you'll have a better understanding of what that means. You can be sure Sergei Fedorov understands that.

———•———————————————•———

Here's Sergei:

I think sports are a great bridge for cultures, for people to understand each other, our mentalities, how we practice, how we train to become a champion—not only between athletes, but between cultures in general.

Even those of us from the Soviet system, we are all different, our ages, even how we play, how we skate, and how we think. But once we got together in Detroit, we figured out our game from the Soviet Union school. That's what happened.

I am glad we did—not once, not twice, but many years in a row. And now we were able to pass on to the next generation, to future hockey players. Maybe make them interested enough to watch what we did and how we played. Maybe pick up a few things.

And we were able to do this in Detroit. I don't think there are many other cities where this could happen, for one reason: the owners. I remember my first year with the Red Wings organization. We received a Christmas catalog from Mr. and Mrs. Ilitch. They treated us as part of their family—and they still do to this day.

When I walk into Joe Louis Arena [more than a dozen years later after that first Stanley Cup celebration], I still feel the same emotional level, same emotions since day one when I walked into that arena. And this kind of success could only happen under their command, Mr. and Mrs. Ilitch. Because they make us a family.

The Vladinator Returns

He said it, didn't he?

"I'll be back."

And when he uttered those words in that thick accent after slipping behind those dark sunglasses, we laughed until it brought us tears.

Now it's just the tears, eh?

But damn if Vladimir Konstantinov didn't recover from horrific injuries that would have killed most of us. He awoke from his weeks-long coma, arose from his hospital bed, and with the help of a walker, got himself from point A to point B on his own two feet. Do you believe in miracles?

"I'll be back."

How can you not believe? On December 31, 2013, the Vladinator made it all the way back, joining a distinguished list of Red Wings alumni who played two games against former Toronto Maple Leafs on a sheet of ice at Comerica Park. It was part of the festivities surrounding the Winter Classic 2014, featuring

Original Six rivals the following day at Michigan Stadium, where the Wings and Leafs shattered the NHL attendance record before 105,491 shivering fans at the Big House.

More important, at least to fans who reveled in those glory days of the late 1990s, Konstantinov's presence marked the first reunion of the Russian Five since they posed for photos at center ice at Joe Louis Arena with the Stanley Cup and other hardware the Wings won that year.

⎯⎯⎯⎯⎯⎯⎯⎯⎯⎯

Nicklas Lidstrom remembers:

It sure meant a lot to me seeing Vladdie back on the ice again with the Russian Five all those years later. He was walking on his own with his walker, and you could tell how happy he was, how happy he was to be back on the ice with his friends that he played with and just able to cherish a moment of being with his Russian teammates again.

I think it says a lot about Vladdie's character, the way he got himself through all the rehab. I remember years after the accident, one of the doctors said that usually when something like this happens you kind of lose your strength. But Vladdie, if you go shake his hand like I did, he still has that strength. He still has that power in his body, and that should've been gone a long time ago.

That just shows his character and determination still. We saw that as a player, but now you see that as a person too, the way he handles himself.

And you know, years after his career was over you can still see the happiness on Vladdie's face at different moments, whether it's getting on the ice again and being cheered by the fans or coming into our locker room the way he used to when I was playing.

He would come in before our warm-up and sit in the locker room for a few minutes and kind of look around. He didn't know many other players. He knew me and maybe a couple of other guys. But just his happiness of being in the locker room again—even if he stayed for only two minutes, he would just sit there and you could sense that he just wanted to get that feeling of being in that room again.

Then he would walk out on the bench and watch our pre-game warm-up. I think he just wanted to be part of all that again and soak it in. It was so great to see him back.

The Last Word

To give credit where credit is due for building the dynasty in Detroit is to recognize a long list of those who deserve it. And make no mistake, this was a dynasty by myriad definitions, beginning with 25 consecutive years qualifying for the post-season, a mark that will never again be reached as long as the NHL imposes a salary cap. Three Stanley Cups in six years, four in a span of 11 seasons. Five President's Trophies in 13 seasons.

That list, of course, begins with Mike and Marian Ilitch, their passion to bring a winner to Detroit and their willingness to do and spend whatever it took to make it happen.

Jim Devellano, the first man the Ilitches hired to be their general manager—and still today the team's senior vice president—started it all with that first draft in 1983 with a list that included Steve Yzerman, Bob Probert, Joe Kocur, and Petr Klima. Devellano hired some of the best scouts in the world who helped find players that made Detroit's 1989 draft the greatest in the history of the NHL.

If you appreciated the likes of Sergei Fedorov, Nick Lidstrom, and Vladimir Konstantinov from that draft, then you can thank former chief scout Neil Smith, his successor Ken Holland, and chief European scouts Christer Rockstrom and Haakan Andersson.

Former coach and assistant GM Nick Polano deserves kudos for his willingness to undertake several crucial cloak-and-dagger missions to help extract players from behind the Iron Curtain. So does Bryan Murray, the coach and GM in the early '90s, when three of those young players began their careers in Detroit.

And then there's Scotty Bowman, the architect of the roster that finally was able to achieve what no Red Wings team had for more than four decades. Noteworthy among his moves were two controversial trades he made for the two older, legendary former Soviet players, Slava Fetisov and Igor Larionov, and two others that landed Brendan Shanahan and Larry Murphy.

Longtime assistants Barry Smith and Dave Lewis deserve mention too. Neither would ever say it out loud, but if you think it was difficult playing for Bowman—and it was, every day, throughout all that success—try serving as one of his assistants. Both men were extremely gracious with their time, never turning down a request to answer a few questions for the media, often at their own peril.

But the final word here goes to Detroit's Oz behind the curtain, the guy who pulled the strings, orchestrating the defections and departures of several players who helped to transform the Detroit Red Wings from a good team to a great team and, eventually, to Stanley Cup champions.

*Then the poor guy wound up running a team in Dallas and, well,
let him tell the story.*

———————————————

Here's Jim Lites:

What the Russian Five did when they played together was fascinating to watch. But by that time I had moved to Dallas—and we were chasing them. We were emulating them. We wanted to become them. We were trying to figure out how to slow those guys down, because we couldn't play with them. They were too good. To be precise, they were too great.

The Russian system that they played had a tremendous impact on how the game was changing in North America, in the NHL. You put those guys with Steve Yzerman, with Nick Lidstrom, and whoever else Kenny Holland and Scotty Bowman and Jimmy Nill put together in the mid '90s, it was really special.

And Scotty Bowman's capability as a coach cannot be underestimated. He was there transforming himself from a hard-core defense-first guy, as evidenced by the Bob Gainey-led Montreal Canadiens in the 1980s, to the Russian Five and an offensive juggernaut. How he evolved as a coach, and coaching those players the way he did, was really special and unique.

But for me, what the Russian Five did was fascinating. In a very short period of time, they acclimated themselves to the North American game. If you watched Vladimir Konstantinov, he looked like he might have been born and raised in London, Ontario. He played like any good North American would play. Slava Kozlov learned to adapt his game. I think he was a relatively shy player when he got here, but he learned to play tougher and to acclimate himself. And Sergei Fedorov, from the very beginning, was just an unbelievably talented, big, strong player. And they were all coachable. They obviously liked being in the system together, and it was truly fascinating.

I helped create that monster, and then I'm in Dallas competing against them, wishing somehow . . . To be honest with you, I had to watch Mr. Ilitch and his team reap the benefits of all that work that had gone into creating it. But still, I had great affection and affinity for the guys themselves because they were hockey players first and foremost.

Petr Klima was the first guy we got [defecting from Czechoslovakia]. He was a great talent, but he wasn't committed to being great. The Russian players that I was involved in getting to Detroit [Fedorov, Konstantinov, and Kozlov] were hockey players, committed guys who cared about the game, about being great. They wanted to win the Stanley Cup. It mattered to them.

And the ability of the five of them together, when they brought in the two older guys with the younger generation getting to play with their own heroes and become the Russian Five, even for that short bit of time, it was amazing and unique.

I had been in Dallas for three years by the time Detroit won that first Stanley Cup, and Mike Ilitch did a really cool thing: he gave me a Stanley Cup ring. I had a 1996-97 Detroit Stanley Cup ring I was given when I was president of the Dallas Stars.

He thanked me for all that I had done while I was there in Detroit, for all the work I had done to build the team, for my work on getting the Russians out of Russia. That really mattered to me.

I was invited to the year-end party, and he gave me that ring, which I was able to give to my grandson, Sam Lites, on his twenty-first birthday. It means a lot to my son to this day.

Acknowledgments

Any list of salutations for this project must begin with my former mentors at the *Detroit Free Press*, starting with retired sports editor Gene Myers and the man he succeeded, Dave Robinson, who rescued me from the newspaper's City Desk to cover the Detroit Red Wings in 1985. The opportunities they provided me, the nurturing support, guidance, and advice along the way, ultimately made this book and the one that preceded it, *The Russian Five*, possible. For them, and for all my colleagues at the Freep across those years, especially on our world-class copy desk, I remain eternally grateful.

I am equally indebted to the Detroit Red Wings' organization, starting with the Ilitch ownership family, which in those years included Jim Lites, now president of the Dallas Stars. He did so much in the early years to orchestrate defections and illicit departures of several players from behind the Iron Curtain, and I especially enjoyed working with him on one particular caper. I remain eternally indebted to former general manager Jim Devellano, who at this writing is in his fortieth season with the franchise, and to several of the coaches he hired, among them Scotty Bowman, Bryan Murray, and Dave Lewis.

Of course, none of this would have been possible without the players—all of them, but in particular Steve Yzerman and such notable teammates as Nicklas Lidstrom, Brendan Shanahan, Kris Draper,

Darren McCarty, Chris Osgood, and the five former Soviet Red Army Club stars who found a new home—as well as a passionate, loving fan following—in Detroit: Sergei Fedorov, Vladimir Konstantinov, Slava Kozlov, Slava Fetisov, and Igor Larionov, in order of their arrival in Hockeytown.

Sadly, the pure rapture they all helped to create with the first Stanley Cup celebration in Detroit 42 years was short-lived because of a limousine accident in which two team members, Konstantinov and massage therapist Sergei Mnatsanakov, sustained devastating injuries that ended their careers. Vladdie—Vlad the Impaler—still requires around-the-clock attention, and it's only appropriate to recognize the many people involved in caring for him, starting with all that former Red Wings trainer John Wharton did for him in the immediate aftermath of the limo crash. That included arranging for the Stanley Cup to be brought to Konstantinov's bedside, an event that helped to bring him out of his weeks-long coma.

Other important people in Vladdie's life: Jim Bellanca, Jr., attorney, family friend, and unabashed Vladimir Konstantinov fan, whose relationship predates the limo crash; Linda Krumm, Vladdie's case manager for two decades and her dedicated, compassionate cadre of caregivers; and Tom Constand, president of the Brain Injury Association of Michigan, who is working tirelessly to reverse Michigan's horrific new insurance law that eviscerates health care coverage for thousands of victims tragically injured in auto accidents, like Vladdie.

I would be remiss not to include the late Dr. John Finley and his wife, Genevieve. It was while working with him on his book *Hockeytown Doc* (Triumph Books, 2012) that I began to think it was possible for me to write my own book. Now there are two, and a third is already well under way.

Finally, my profound respect, admiration, and appreciation to The

Russian Five franchise team: Dan Milstein, the executive producer of the award-winning documentary film whose company published my first book; his consigliere Jenny Feterovich; and director Joshua Riehl, who hit a grand-slam home run with his first major project. It was an honor to be part of that team, serving as writer/producer of an extraordinary film that still brings tears to my eyes every time I see it.